PARAPSYCHOLOGY
and the Christian Faith

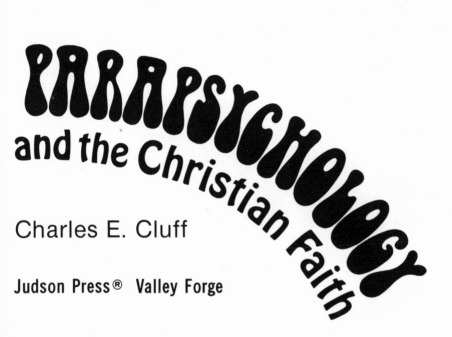

PARAPSYCHOLOGY
and the Christian Faith

Charles E. Cluff

Judson Press® Valley Forge

Library of Congress Cataloging in Publication Data

Cluff, Charles E.
　Parapsychology and the Christian faith.

　Bibliography: p. 113.
　1. Christianity and psychical research. I. Title.
BR115.P85C58　　201'.9　　76-25015
ISBN 0-8170-0715-6

TO BETTY, MARK, and CARRIE

ACKNOWLEDGMENTS

I express my sincere appreciation to San Francisco Theological Seminary for their doctoral program. I thank Mrs. Eleanor Ives for the help in typing and most of all thank my family for their patience and willingness to "let me go" for awhile to do this project.

CONTENTS

INTRODUCTION

I have always had a real interest in new ideas in all kinds of fields: in physics, medicine, psychology, astronomy, geology, and other fields or disciplines. I have a large file, which comes from articles or books with which I have come in contact, that contains new research material in each of these disciplines. Parapsychology is a relatively new discipline and I find myself drawn to it. My interest in new ideas relates to my faith, too, for I believe God to be extremely contemporary. He is the "I am" of every present moment; in fact, he is probably the only One able to be completely in the present.

My exposure to the field of parapsychology occurred through a number of different personal experiences. You will read about some of them in this book. I believe that the discoveries in this field of expanding research and awareness are absolutely amazing in themselves and have more wide-reaching spiritual implications than any other present discipline, possibly with the exception of theology. I say "possibly" with the exception of theology because, if theology means how God fits into a formally determined doctrinal framework, many people around me don't seem to be very much interested.

The December, 1973, issue of *Psychology Today* contained an extensive religious survey. The survey was not to determine the doctrinal beliefs of the readers, but the spiritual interest of the readers. A comment in the introduction of the survey indicated the possibility that in the past people were going to church but were not religious, and that today people seem to be very religious but are not going to church. The results of the survey have revealed that this does seem to be true.

In the field of parapsychology there are many people involved who are very religious, but in a way that is mostly nontraditional. They are interested in the universe as a spiritual universe. The material they are dealing with and the areas they are researching have tremendous implications for Christianity. What they are discovering is aiding the understanding of many occurrences within Christian phenomena, such as spiritual healing.

The material contained in this book may be used for individual reading or for small-group study. I have used it in churches, during the educational hour, the evening Bible study hour, and in small home-study groups. It is interesting as individual reading but even more helpful as a focus for group interaction and discussion.

This material is designed to expose Christians who are already interested in some aspects of parapsychology to the wider field of parapsychology. It seeks to suggest how Christians might consider traditional Christian beliefs in a different way. The book is organized into six chapters. The first chapter introduces parapsychology, gives a bit of its background, and presents a possible rationale for Christians who are interested in the subject to deal further with it. The second chapter conveys a general picture of discoveries being made by parapsychological research. The third chapter presents Kirlian photography and the amazing discovery of energy bodies that coexist with our physical-material bodies. It also shows some of the implications of this discovery. The fourth chapter deals with occurrences within the field of parapsychology, of phenomena that seem to happen due to outside entity involvement. (The words "entity, " "being," and "person" are all synonymous in this writing; entity is the most common word used within parapsychological circles. All of them refer to a consciously existent "self," an independently thinking and acting being.) It deals with the biblical picture of outside entities as either angels or demons. Chapter 5 is the largest division, for it contains a possible cosmology from a Christian viewpoint that in consideration of what the previous chapters have revealed might be embraced, that is open to what is occurring and is also, in the author's viewpoint, faithful to the message of the gospel. The last chapter develops some concepts of the mind as it relates to faith and our becoming. Questions after each chapter can be used for individual consideration or group discussion if desired.

I have spent months researching, thinking, and praying about these concepts and thus by now have a "feel" for them. As the reader you may be overwhelmed if this is your first exposure to some of these new areas. This material, though, seems to have enriched the lives of many of the believers who have been in different groups where I have shared many of these concepts and they have been discussed.

All of us are unique, I am aware, and are therefore at different places in our growth and development. Not everyone may be interested in the same areas of this book. I am convinced, however, that in most Christian circles there are groups of individuals who are in a disposition conducive to this kind of further exposure. It is for them that this material can be helpful. In every church with which I have participated there have been believers not only interested in the phenomena discussed but also involved. Many who are having extrasensory perception (ESP) experiences and other happenings are looking for more of a possible Christian understanding of them.

It is my hope that this book will be as meaningful to you as its preparation has been to me. It is really just an introduction to a field others will certainly wish to continue exploring.

Chapter I

PARAPSYCHOLOGY INTRODUCED

In this chapter I wish to specify further the purpose and intended use of this material. After this I will define "parapsychology," differentiate between psychic phenomena and the occult, and discuss what we may do with something new.

The purpose of this book is to aid believers who are interested in and opening up to parapsychological phenomena to understand a possible Christian framework for their new awareness. The intention is not to try to persuade anyone to believe in the subject. This is not an apologetic for or a defense of parapsychology. The material presented here may serve to solidify the reader's feelings about certain "paranormal" experiences, but attempting to convert one to belief would possibly be an immense task and it is not the undertaking of this book. This is important to remember, for the discussions presuppose the reader's awareness of and openness to certain phenomena not traditionally explained by science. I will give a general, overall picture of the major areas of consideration for the purpose of expanding the reader's awareness, but not for the purpose of persuasion. Understanding or acceptance must come from individual belief.

This book is for persons wanting to understand how parapsychology might relate to their faith. Some people are saying that Christianity and parapsychology are not compatible. I believe they are, and this book seeks to show this compatibility. I have conducted seminars in several churches, and within each church I have found a number of people interested in the subject. I found that most individuals who participated also have had some experiences of unusual awareness and occurrences between themselves and relatives or close friends, such as feeling something being wrong before knowing it objectively. They wished to understand these things in light of their Christian faith. This book was developed for such people.

Parapsychology Explained

Parapsychology is a division of psychology that investigates what some people are now calling "paranormal" phenomena. *Webster's Third New International Dictionary* defines parapsychology as: "a science concerned with the investigation, especially by experimental means, of events that are apparently not accounted for by natural law and that are considered to be evidence of mental telepathy, clairvoyance, and psychokinesis."

Natural law in this dictionary definition would refer to "known" natural laws. As new understanding develops, new laws will develop; and as they stand the test of time, they will be called "natural." Previously unknown laws are now being defined and some day will probably be accepted as normal or natural by scientists all over the world.

Parapsychology describes the branch of science that grew out of the study of psychic phenomena. The study of such phenomena was first known as psychical research. The shorthand designation for the field of psychic phenomena is the Greek letter "psi." Paranormal is the description of events that are beyond what present scientific categories define as normal.

Any great body of knowledge or collection of facts amassed by observation and experimentation and tested for adherence to some general truth or law is called a science. Science, you might say, is knowledge reduced to law and embodied in a system. The scientific aspects of parapsychology in the United States began at Duke University in the early 1930s under the leadership of J. B. Rhine. Dr. Rhine is often referred to as the "father of parapsychology." Early experiments involved the testing of ESP in a laboratory setting; the results with certain psychic people consistently bettered chance. Psychic people are individuals who seem to acquire information and have experiences through means other than the five senses. Dr. Rhine's book *The Reach of the Mind* gives the best picture of the earliest experiments and results of the treatment of parapsychology as a science.

The pioneers in the field of parapsychology labored under great skepticism from their peers, and it was only on December 30, 1969, that the Parapsychological Association was admitted into the American Association for the Advancement of Science. Since that time it has held the status of a legitimate science in this very respectable body of scientists in the United States. As a science, parapsychology is seeking to understand, explain, and systematize phenomena that are definitely occurring consistently in laboratory settings.

Psychic Phenomena and the Occult

The term "parapsychology" is a more inclusive word than "psychic phenomenon" or the "occult." Psychic refers mainly to the mind and spirit, the psyche. This term refers to the soul or spirit as distinguished from the body. Parapsychology deals not only with the mind and spirit (or soul) but also with the body and with the interrelatedness among all three. Parapsychology is aware of and seeks to understand and explain the interrelatedness of all in existence, whether mind, spirit, or matter.

Parapsychology is distinguished from the occult because the term "occult" refers basically to that which is hidden or mysterious. It has the connotation to many of being a negative word referring to or being associated mainly with spiritism or demonism, or contacting and talking with the dead. Dr. Milan Ryzl, who teaches parapsychological courses at universities in the Bay Area in Northern California, defines the occult as being

> . . . based on a system of beliefs, or even superstitions, whereas the goal of the parapsychologist has always been to use scientific methods to investigate unknown laws of nature. . . . "parapsychology" . . . is really a separate branch of science which is as close to physics as it is to psychology. And it is also related to all the other branches: anthropology, mathematics, religion, biology.[1]

Many Christians I know seem to be aware of the occult aspects of parapsychology. This is because of the amount of attention that has been given to the increased interest of many in witchcraft and astrology. Many Christian and non-Christian articles have been written that show large numbers of people involved in these two specific areas of parapsychological activity. An example is the statement by William G. Roll, project director of The Psychical Research Foundation in Durham: "We are experiencing an upsurge of interest in the occult. Newspaper and magazine articles constantly attest to this." John Godwin, journalist and author of *Occult America,* sees a wave of mysticism coming to America.[2] Samuel McCracken, an editor of *Change* and assistant professor of literature and humanities at Reed College, says he sees a "growing and uncritical admiration for and acceptance of the esoteric and the occult. . . ."[3] Harvey Brooks, dean of the Division of Engineering and Applied Physics at Harvard, says that there is

. . . a flight toward antirational cults. Astrology, once the refuge of the ignorant and the illiterate, is now gaining favor among many intellectuals, even young scientists . . . the national investment in astrology is between ten and twenty times that in astronomy.[4]

Alvin Toffler, writer and visiting scholar at the Russell Sage Foundation, speaks in *Future Shock* of a "garish revival of mysticism."[5]

Trends magazine reports:

Increasing numbers of people are turning, with greater or lesser seriousness, to a study of astrology, psychic phenomena, and other occult pursuits. Even computers have become involved, with at least two firms casting detailed horoscopes by means of the wizardry of IBM. The *New York Times* reports the existence of some 400 witch covens throughout the U.S. Colleges and high schools are offering courses in witchcraft.[6]

A great many serious, rational, and sensible people are caught up in the world of the occult, living their lives by one or more of its manifestations.

Parapsychology includes the occult, to be sure, but it is one very small aspect of a very wide range of areas of concern, and there are sane and serious researchers, individuals, and organizations working to bring the many positive aspects of parapsychological research to the public for application and use for the betterment of humankind. Some of these individuals are devout believers in Christ and in the gospel. They are experiencing frustration as they find that many nonbelievers are much more open to what they believe God is leading persons to discover than believers.

It seems as though more and more people are becoming aware of the larger field of psychic phenomena. My observations concur with those of Richard Neff, author of *Psychic Phenomena and Religion* and pastor of the Christian Community Presbyterian Church of Bowie, Maryland, who noticed, while preparing his book, "a rapidly growing interest in psychic phenomena."[7] Some professionals in the field of psychology are beginning to open up to these changes. Richard Neff observes that psychologists attempt to fit unusual psychic phenomena into current categories of their own disciplines, where the parapsychologist searches for new categories and different theories beyond current psychological theory to understand and describe these events.[8] In my reading, however, I find this not to be as true with some psychologists today as it might have been just a few years ago. I mention here some of the things that are being said today by some psychological researchers. There is a new awareness of the complexity of human beings and of their being much more than they were previously thought to be. A growing number of psychologists seem to be aware of this.

Robert Ornstein is a research psychologist at Langley Porter Neuropsychiatric Institute. He also teaches at the University of California Medical Center in San Francisco. Ornstein is a graduate of Queens College of the City University of New York and of Stanford University, California. In 1969 he received the American Institutes of Research Creative Talent Award. In his appraisal of the things occurring in the field of psychology, he states several provocative ideas that indicate new and meaningful awarenesses in the field. In his book *The Psychology of Consciousness* Ornstein indicates his feelings that it is time for students of psychology and science in the West to use modern psychological terms to describe some of the theories of traditional psychologies and thus to regain a balance he feels has been lost. To do this, though, he thinks we must adjust the boundaries of research in modern science to include new possibilities for humankind. If there can be a change, then there will be a redefinition of the terms "normal" and "paranormal." He compares this change with the breaking of the four-minute mile which opened new areas of running possibility. He feels we are just in the first few moments of the new synthesis that is allowing an extended concept of humankind to emerge. He enumerates that he thinks the elements of this new synthesis are: (1) The awareness of the fact that two major modes of consciousness exist in humankind, and that they function in a complementary manner. (2) We are beginning to focus our attention, both personal and scientific, on discovering the nature of consciousness itself and on internal self-control. (3) Contrary to what Western scientists thought, humankind is not a completely closed system. (4) The concepts of "normal" and "paranormal" are changing.[9]

Related to psychology's discovery that the person has nonphysical realities, J. B. Rhine states: "There now is evidence that such an extraphysical factor exists in man."[10] He further states:

> The discovery of a nonphysical psi factor then introduces psychology to a new area to be explored in search of the principles that make people do what they do; for powers and processes that are personal, not physical; for properties of living beings that are psychical, not material.[11]

Rhine also believes that "it is now fairly clear that psi phenomena are identified by the fact that they defy physical explanation and require a psychological one."[12]

Carl Jung, the famous Swiss psychiatrist and psychologist, makes an appraisal of Western psychology. Referring to the general perspective of the psychological approach in the past, he indicates that our Western psychology is a "science of mere phenomena without any metaphysical implications." He adds that the "development of Western philosophy during the last two centuries has . . . [isolated] the mind in its own sphere and [has succeeded] in severing it from its primordial oneness with the universe."[13]

This picture seems to be changing today, and the change is well expressed by Claudio Naranjo. In his book *The One Quest* he suggests that psychiatry and psychology have two ideas in common with the religious view: There is a basic wrongness in the average person's condition and persons are involved in a development process which extends beyond their school years. He feels that the therapist has come to recognize that even when the wrongness in a patient's life has been corrected, he or she still experiences an emptiness which he or she wants to have filled. This need cannot be fulfilled by material possessions, family life, or work.[14]

Naranjo sees psychology and psychiatry as beginning to recognize that persons are spiritual beings, or mystical beings, who have needs to be met which are more than those traditionally recognized by some therapists. He points out that in terms of the Freudian ideas about "sublimation of libidinal impulses, mysticism could be regarded as a flight from reality, a substitution of 'God' for the immediate objects of desire and a form of wish fulfillment in fantasy and symbol rather than actuality." However, Naranjo sees the mystic's view as just the opposite. He regards the earthly things persons desire as substitutes for what they really want. He states that all our longings originate, whether we know it or not, from our longing for God, and what we go after in the form of different objects is based on the assumption that we will find what we seek in them.[15]

The awareness of the mystical is an awareness of the psychical too—that is, that persons are more than what is traditionally thought of as "psychological." Thus, many who are studying parapsychology are called parapsychologists. It is, in my opinion, only a matter of time until the discoveries of parapsychology will be common recognitions and regularly used principles of established psychology and psychiatry.

We know today that psychic phenomena can be observed in controlled laboratory conditions. Informed persons are no longer skeptical about significant occurrences of a number of "out of the ordinary" happenings. Dr. Allen Cohen, a clinical psychologist in Berkeley and director of the Drug Abuse Institute of the John F. Kennedy University in Martinez, speaks of three traditional types of psychic phenomena: mind to mind, mind to matter, and matter to mind. I would also include energy. Matter, energy, and mind are separate awarenesses that are being observed and studied by parapsychologists.

Things are occurring between minds, between minds and matter, between matter and matter, and between energy and minds and matter that seem to necessitate a radical change in our scientific view of humankind. Richard Neff states his feeling that the "acceptance of the concept of ESP" (a general description of the things just mentioned) does require "some basic rethinking and restructuring of one's concept of the universe."[16] These changes of thinking may have tremendous spiritual implications for the Christian. It is likely that it will be easier than ever before for most of us as believers to talk about the soul, spirit, afterlife and God.

Phenomena under consideration by parapsychologists include items such as telepathy; biofeedback; hypnotism; faith healing; precognition; psychokinesis; auras around plants, animals, and people; brain control; out-of-body experiences; astrology, eyeless sight; acupuncture; witchcraft; prophecy; and what we naively call ESP. This is just a partial list.

Something New

I love 2 Timothy 1:7 which says, "God hath not given us the spirit of fear; but of power, and of love, and of a sound mind."

As Christians we are conscientious about what we believe. We want to honor God with our thoughts and actions. But sometimes we seem too hesitant to consider "new things" that might be different from the faith we feel God wants us to embrace. What we may often mean by the faith we feel God wants us to have, though, is the faith we were *taught* to have, or that we are used to and with which we are comfortable.

It brings to my mind the many things I believe and feel I understand right now that I didn't even know about, much less believe existed, just a few years ago. God is more real and exciting to me than at any other time and is in the process of constantly reshaping my understanding of him and the gospel. I have not changed what I believe the Christian faith means but am finding new ways to express it to our growing and expanding world. These "new ways" are enriching my faith a great deal.

How do we, or how should we, as Christians deal with something that is new to us? I purposefully said "new to us" because the material under consideration is not new. In fact, it is very old. Acupuncture goes back to at least some 2,000 years B.C., and the Bible shows us that a large number of occurrences now classified under parapsychology were existent in earliest Old Testament days. For example, the practice of mediums is mentioned early in the Old Testament.

There may be nothing new under the sun, but what is new, however, is the sophisticated level on which research is being conducted to explain these phenomena. What is new is the acceptance of these things by Iron Curtain countries that don't claim to believe in God, and by the Western world's intellectuals who are not given to superstition or fantasy. Physicians, physicists, chemists, and scientists of all kinds are exploring areas of reality previously bypassed as nonsense and which they now consider to be reasonable, logical, and sensible. Non-Christians are believing in healing, for example, while some Christians are still arguing among themselves whether God is doing healing today. While some believers are still discussing the different "gifts" mentioned in Corinthians, secular researchers are watching these gifts working in laboratory settings.

As previously mentioned, the thoughts and ideas contained in this study have been presented to several groups of Christians.

Occasionally the question has arisen: "Why should we bother with any of this?" It is because interest in parapsychology does not seem to be just a fad. As Dr. William Tiller, professor of Material Science at Stanford University, says:

> "When an idea's time has come, nothing on earth can stop it!" Well, we are at that moment in time when such an event is happening—a transformation is occurring in man! Future mankind will probably look back and say that the beginning of the Psychic Age of Man occurred around the early 1970s.[17]

If this is true, or even partially true, there will be Christians who feel they must deal with this material on a level tantamount to the sophistication of the researchers now in this field. If Christians continue to associate parapsychology solely with occultism and instruct the church to stay clear of the whole field of para-psychological phenomena—which is exploring the interrelatedness of minds, energies, etc.—informed individuals may eventually question the responsibility of Christianity.

We are seeing real things happening, and some Christians feel the need to deal with this new awareness and understanding of life. A woman in a church told me she was scared by those discoveries and didn't want to know about them. It may be easier sometimes not to know about something because then we don't have to make up our minds about it. If we open ourselves up to face a problem, then we have to come to a decision about it.

We might be able to bypass articles in newspapers and magazines and can possibly refuse to read books on the subject, or stay away from lectures and programs; but we may find it difficult to ignore things we feel or the questions posed by college students taking courses in parapsychology. The March 4, 1974, *Time* magazine states that more than one hundred colleges in the United States are offering courses in parapsychology. There are most likely at least double that today.

Parapsychology is an empirical phenomenon today. It is relying on observation and experimentation. To ignore it or let it bypass us is possibly to overlook what God may be revealing to us today. There are new facts we have to deal with that may cause us to do some strenuous thinking and mental and spiritual adjusting.

A World View

One of the disciplines I have been involved in is the working through and rethinking of my world view. For example, are we to see the world as a friendly place wherein God is leading us in the ascending to himself, as the kingdom of heaven comes on earth even as it is in heaven, or is the world basically influenced by a satanic being that is trying to take us further and further down? These, of course, are two opposite extremes, but if the latter is true, then maybe there should be a real hesitancy and fear related to our new discoveries about ourselves. If the former theory is true, then one would probably see God's working in the movements of the world and prayerfully seek to see how it can help us know more about God, his will, and his working. We are also really talking about eschatology, and we all are aware that there are some very astute and dedicated Christian theologians on both sides of the world view extremes just mentioned, each supporting scripturally the position he or she holds.

The phenomena I will be referring to may seem rather amazing if this is the first time you have been exposed to them. Parapsychological experiments are really quite mind expanding. They may stimulate your imagination to activity which used to be considered fantasy dreaming; but then when you see these phenomena occurring under controlled laboratory settings, you will probably lean toward considering them "for real." Now what, though? What do we do with this new material we are just beginning to recognize and understand?

Some people may pretend it isn't happening, but that works for only a short time. If something is "truth," it eventually has to be encountered. Some call parapsychology "of Satan." Many Christians think this way about psychic phenomena. After speaking at Castle Air Force Base, having made references to things occurring in parapsychology, I received a note from a concerned Christian that said:

> There were many things you alluded to that day that led me to believe you are allowing yourself to become involved in parapsychology. I normally would have shrugged this off as a passing fancy, but the Holy Spirit will not let me do so. I have been praying for you since that day and now feel I must speak out to you about parapsychology.

She then quoted some verses that specifically referred to mediums, wizards, etc. In my hometown there have been meetings drawing large crowds of people—meetings that deal with the evils of parapsychology and the occult. One approach, then, is to consider these phenomena satanic. (Some aspects of it may be negative, to be sure, but the negative is just a part of the total picture.)

Another response to the discovery and the upsurge of interest in parapsychology is to see God as leading and guiding persons into a further awareness of their reality. This is my feeling, and along with it is the belief that all truth is neutral. That is, what is, is, and we make it either good or bad. We are discovering new natural laws today that apparently have always been working, but now they are being revealed in a new light and, as we see them more clearly, we can use them more fully. They may be the phenomena seen throughout the Bible, and particularly in the life of Jesus, which we had thought were supernatural. Now we may begin seeing these happenings as quite "natural." I have long believed that Jesus showed us the potential of all persons if they could be attuned to God as he was. Everything he did may have been natural for human beings and would be seen in all persons if they were one with God as he was.

Romans 14:14 declares firmly the apostle Paul's belief that all things are neutral in themselves—neither good nor bad until we take hold of them. We seem to make things good or bad by attitudes and our use of God's world. Parapsychology is disclosing more natural data that is bad if it is used for evil—but good if it is used for good. Black witchcraft, for example, would be an evil use of psychic phenomena. Gifts such as we see in the New Testament are good uses of what we are calling "psychic phenomena" or "parapsychological phenomena."

We may not feel comfortable referring to spiritual gifts in this kind of a human way, but I am more convinced than ever that there is no distinction between the spiritual and the natural. Natural law is good, as God has made all that exists good. We are either spiritual or nonspiritual in what we do with God's world. Thus, from our own use of God's world, we seem to make that which God created as "the way it is" either good or bad. This involves the way the material world is, the way the energy world is, and the way the mental world is. We are discovering some "natural laws" that are not physical and material that can be used to help or hinder humankind.

As science comes up with new laws that seem to explain the nonphysical-nonmaterial world, it may be our witness not to oppose them but to understand them in light of God's revelation of himself. It is ours to pray for the leading of God's spirit in helping to interpret what these discoveries can mean to humankind. It is ours also to warn of the consequences of their misuse.

There is a misuse, and parapsychologists are becoming more and more aware of it. The dangers relate to every area from mind training to out-of-body experiences to the practice of mediumism. Elmer and Alyce Green, noted biofeedback researchers at the Menninger Foundation in Topeka, Kansas, see mind-training courses as potentially dangerous. In a report written for the Academy of Parapsychology and Medicine, they contend that some courses induce in some persons a form of paranoid neurosis or psychosis, often related to obsession or possession. They continue to say that one cannot go beyond his or her own rate of natural development and maturity without negative effects.

Some researchers feel there will be profoundly disturbing effects occurring in people who get "over their heads" in their experiences. It has been suggested by some that we will have to become as discriminating about most alternatives to drugs as we are now with the drugs themselves. It is believed that through improper use of alternate consciousness states, such as meditation, out-of-body travel, etc., confusion will occur as people have experiences they cannot integrate properly into their life views. We may soon be treating many who cannot pull themselves back together. An example might be the number who already think they are obsessed.

The positive aspects of what we are discovering have tremendous salutary ramifications, though, and it is these aspects that researchers are seeking to discover and disclose. Robert Mattson, of the Academy of Parapsychology and Medicine, expresses this in his statement of the purpose of this academy as "learning to make our psychic powers work for the goal of mankind." He states that part of the organization's goals is to convince medicine that these powers exist and are helpful and must be used.

There is one particularly fine benefit coming from the "psychic revolution" we are breaking into—that is, that many people who are more psychic than normal are finding out they are not mentally ill. Since my interest in parapsychology has spread around the immediate area of my hometown, I have had several people, many of them Christians, set up appointments and share with me experiences they would have been put in mental institutions for telling anyone just a few years ago. I believe we will find that we have persecuted many psychic individuals by institutionalizing them, individuals who merely needed help in understanding what their unusual experiences meant. I feel we need a psychic liberation. I think people should know they are normal when they hear voices and experience visions. We need to understand and accept that psychic experience is not unnatural and is not an illness.

Let me, in passing, call your attention to the Bible, to the fact that the hearing of voices and the seeing of visions is a recurring phenomenon. Research today is affirming many biblical happenings, but it is also putting these occurrences in categories other than spiritual. What the church has traditionally thought of as being directly of God (referring to God's specific activity) or directly of Satan may be just the way God has created humankind and the universe we live in. These parapsychological discoveries will some day be put into clear systems that will be as common as the physical-material laws we have today.

The past world of parapsychological phenomena has been a flat world, such as our physical world was thought to be years ago. There are many who have sailed across the unknown and who have found that world round and real and friendly. Some individuals still seem to believe it is flat, but it is only a matter of time until its roundness will be accepted. The Christian must be there to help all the manifestations find meaning and service to God.

Richard Neff thinks that "an open-minded investigation of psychic phenomena will confirm many of the traditional teachings of Christianity." He suggests that parapsychological findings will support the possibilities of life after death, spiritual healing, and prayer.[18] I believe this, too, and am more impressed every day with what I think of as the magnificent plan of God being worked in the world today. We should be observant, prayerful, and open, for if it is of God that we are discovering these new categories of his existence, we will not be able to ignore them. If we do, we might even be found to be opposing God (Acts 5:39).

It might be a good exercise at this juncture to think clearly about your present attitude toward parapsychology and the list of phenomena mentioned on page 21. How much do you know about each one of the items and how do you explain those with which you are acquainted? If you do have an opinion, where did you develop it? Is it your opinion or that of others? Are you open to new things you might learn and experience, or does the "unknown" scare or threaten you? What is your world view? Do you see the world as friendly or hostile? Do you see "spiritual" things as separate categories or as humankind's use of God's natural phenomena? Are things good or bad in themselves or do we make them so?

Chapter II

EXAMPLES OF PARAPSYCHOLOGICAL PHENOMENA

This chapter is intended to provide the reader with a general overview of some of the types of phenomena being explored today and to give some samples of the research taking place in the use of them. It will be a survey rather than an exhaustive treatment of the areas discussed. The object is to expose the reader to several categories being seriously researched. The discussion will cover just a partial list of phenomena being examined by researchers today. There will not necessarily be an interconnectedness or order among the categories. Certain ones were chosen simply because they demonstrate areas we need to think about.

I want to emphasize again that the intent is not to persuade or convince the reader to accept all of the data included. The emphasis is on serious research. Some of you may question whether a certain phenomenon I will discuss has been thoroughly proven. I do not feel the weight of having to prove the findings but rather to convey that they are occurring enough to justify serious empirical examination and investigation. There is enough evidence to keep persons seriously conducting experimentation and examination, and enough evidence to cause some very responsible intellectuals to affirm publicly the validity of these phenomena.

If you wish to acquire a detailed awareness of the field of parapsychological phenomena and the research being done today, I recommend that you read *Psychic Discoveries Behind the Iron Curtain* by Sheila Ostrander and Lynn Schroeder (1970). Other books that will give a good introduction to and overview of parapsychology are *ESP Research Today* by J. G. Pratt (1973)—Dr. Pratt is a well-known parapsychologist who was associated for many years with the Duke University Parapsychology Laboratory and is now an Associate Professor of Psychiatry at the University of Virginia School of Medicine—and *Parapsychology Today,* Parapsychology Foundation, New York (1973). The latter book is a survey that stresses a geographic approach to parapsychology and covers what is happening in many different countries; it is edited by Allan Angoff and Betty Shapin. Edgar Mitchell, the sixth man on the moon, has published a book called *Psychic Exploration.* It is an overview of the whole field. For further information you may also wish to write to two organizations: the Academy of Parapsychology and Medicine in Palo Alto, California, and the Institute of Noetic Sciences, also in Palo Alto. They will make available to you other current data about the scope, investigation, and places of research.

The phenomena I will discuss are just a few of the happenings that seem to be encouraging science to consider changing some of its traditional views of the world. If the phenomena become "accepted" occurrences, we will probably all be involved in rethinking a number of things. As Christians, we may be reevaluating some of our traditional interpretations of the universe and how God has made it and what it means to be a part of it.

Extrasensory Perception

Extrasensory perception refers generally to things occurring that involve awareness coming from other than our five senses. This is a broad term that includes a number of other phenomena, such as telepathy and clairvoyance. Probably everyone has experienced something that could be called "ESP." My wife and her mother always seem to know when the other is ill by some form of intuition; it relates to hunches that have turned out to be accurate. Recently the news media carried the story of a boy who "felt" different about an automobile covered with snow. He got help and a woman was found pinned in it; she had been there for forty-five hours. Such unusual feelings are being studied in ESP research.

In an interview with John Brodie, quarterback for the San Francisco 49ers for over sixteen years, *Intellectual Digest* related an aspect of psychic phenomena occurring in some sport experiences. John Brodie states: "Sometimes I let the ball fly before Gene [Washington] has made his final move, without a pass route." [1] On numerous occasions, what they both did without a conscious awareness of the other's activity coincided perfectly.

There are many examples of ESP; some may be your own.

Telepathy

Telepathy is a designation of the ability to send or receive messages from mind to mind without the use of visual or verbal tools. This can be done hundreds of miles apart. The Russians have done some very fine experimentation in this area, and Dr. Douglas Dean, president of the New Jersey Society of the Parapsychological Association, says they have actually photographed this phenomenon; this was done with Kirlian photography which will be discussed later. When telepathy is fully developed, a person can consciously send thoughts to another person, who can consciously receive the thoughts.

In 1966 Dr. Dean demonstrated that telepathy can be transmitted to a person who is not even aware the transmission is taking place. This is reported in the *International Journal of Neuropsychiatry.* He showed, with measuring instruments, that a subject's blood vessels contracted when another person in a room 250 yards away concentrated on a thought emotionally meaningful to the subject. This occurred with enough consistency as to rule out coincidence.

A major part of the research being done with telepathy is related to dreams. Dr. Stanley Krippner, psychologist, is head of the research team at Maimonides Medical Center's Dream Laboratory in New York City. He is one of the best-known researchers in telepathy and dreaming. Dr. Krippner is one of the authors of the book *Dream Telepathy,* which conveys some of their findings in dream research as related to telepathy. This is basically how the research was set up. The experimental subject was brought into the laboratory in the evening to become familiar with the laboratory. The subject was then prepared for sleep and electrodes were fastened to his scalp. He went to sleep. By what are called "REMs" or rapid eye movements, researchers could tell when he was dreaming. The brain wave movements were also noted on the equipment. When the records showed the subject was dreaming, they woke him up and asked him to tell what he had been dreaming. In another room almost a hundred feet away another person was sending thoughts to the sleeping person. The dream was checked out and compared to the thoughts that had been beamed to him from the other person. Later the data was compared and the results were indicated on the record. Over the years, the results have been significantly better than chance. Stanley Krippner relates that enough has been done to show that in a span of a half-dozen years with over a hundred subjects there has been a significant relation between what is "sent" and what is "received." [2]

It is fairly common knowledge that everyone dreams. Some remember their dreams and others do not. Furthermore, Krippner feels that persons possess a latent capacity for ESP which is most likely to be deployed when a person dreams during sleep. He also feels that PSI is not a gift of only those rare persons who are psychically sensitive but can be experienced by almost everyone under the right conditions.[3] He also believes the soul can project itself into all kinds of experiences and return to impress these memories upon the mind at the moment of waking. Dr. Krippner further comments that of all the states of consciousness investigated by parapsychological researchers as being most conducive to ESP, dreaming is the only one that we experience every day, which occurs in regular intervals, about every ninety minutes during a night's sleep.[4] If their conclusions are accurate, we all are involved in the phenomenon of mental telepathy every time we sleep.

Some experts in the field have suggested that this form of communication will be necessary for space travel, for there does not seem to be a time or space effect on telepathy. It is instantaneous. This particular fact is not understood, for previously everything we have known has been within a time-space construct.

Biofeedback

Biofeedback, or personal mind control, is a process wherein persons can monitor their own physiology in areas or on levels usually below or outside of their normal awareness. Persons are finding that they can control with their minds what was traditionally thought of as part of our autonomic systems, and thus not affected by the conscious mind.

This process involves the mind's control of the physical body. Science now distinguishes between four major brain-wave frequencies. Each is associated with a certain state of mind and a corresponding physiological state. The four areas are: *Beta,* 13 cycles per second and above, which is associated with ordinary work activity, such as reading or other focused attention; *Alpha,* 8-12 CPS, which is associated with a quiet, objective state of mind, a calm, relaxed, and meditative state free from anxiety; *Theta,* 4-7 CPS, associated with deep meditation and moments of highest inspiration, creativity, and problem solving; *Delta,* 0.5-3 CPS, which is the slowest brain wave and which occurs in deep, dreamless sleep, a state normally without consciousness.

All persons produce these major brain-wave patterns at different intervals during their daily cycle. As brain-wave patterns change, the ability to perform daily activities changes as well.

One can learn to control the various brain-wave patterns. This is the goal of biofeedback. The first step is to be aware of these levels. The second is to learn to control them, and the third is to learn to control them in outside settings, in everyday life settings. Methods of control have been established in university laboratory work.

Human functioning, such as thought, blood flow, and heart rate, can be brought under the influence of the will. People can learn to regulate heartbeat, lower blood pressure, forestall an asthma attack, avoid a migraine headache, control the mental state, and redirect the blood flow or supply to raise or lower body temperature. Some people are conceiving of a future time when one can kill one's own tumors and other illnesses or growths that live by blood flow simply by consciously stopping the flow of blood to that part.

Biofeedback research is making us realize that we have been grossly underestimating the potential of human beings. Robert Ornstein reports the results of a study conducted at the Menninger Foundation by Elmer Green. During this study a yoga master showed that he was able to raise the temperature at one point on his hand while at the same time he lowered the temperature at another point on the same hand. The difference in temperature between the two points at the end of the experiment was 11 degrees. Ornstein also mentions other reports which demonstrate that yogis can control their flow of blood and their blood pressure. They can also "lower their basal metabolic rate by more than 15 percent" for long periods of time.[5]

There is a lot of enthusiasm about the possibilities of this phenomenon. Andrew Weil expresses it as follows:

> The possibility that one can learn to influence directly such "involuntary" functions as heart rate, blood pressure, blood flow in internal

organs, endocrine secretions, and perhaps even cellular processes by conscious use of the autonomic nervous system is the most exciting frontier of modern medicine.[6]

There is a Biofeedback Research Society. Dr. Barbara Brown, director of Experiential Physiology at the Veteran's Hospital in Supulveda, California, was co-founder. Doctors Elmer and Alyce Green are doing extensive research at the Menninger Foundation in the field of biofeedback.

Alternate Consciousness States

Another development that strongly relates to the mind can be classified under the category of alternate consciousness states. This basically deals with the mind being able to lead one to experience reality that is not physical or material. Sleep and daydreaming are examples of altered states of consciousness, as are trance, hypnosis, meditation, general anesthesia, delirium, psychosis, mystic rapture, and the various chemical "highs." Possibly the best way to understand this category may be through the picture of a real dream or daydream, or an imaginary mental picture being "real" in its own dimension. Your daydream, for example, may be a real experience that is not physical or material. If you want to get a good look at this aspect of parapsychology, you might want to read *The Center of the Cyclone,* by John Lilly, or *The Natural Mind,* by Andrew Weil. There are others, but these will give you an exposure to the concepts entertained in this category. John C. Lilly is a graduate of the California Institute of Technology and received his doctorate in medicine from the University of Pennsylvania in 1942. He spent twelve years working on research on dolphin-human relationships, including communications, and two years at Esalen Institute, Big Sur, California, as a group leader, resident, and associate in residence. His previous books are *Man and Dolphin, The Mind of the Dolphin,* and *Programming and Metaprogramming in the Human Biocomputer.* A *New York Times'* book review called him a "walking one-man syllabus of Western civilization." Dr. Lilly has worked extensively in various research fields of science, including biophysics, paraphysiology, electronics, and neuroanatomy. He says that it is his "firm belief that the experience of higher states of consciousness is necessary for survival of the human species."[7]

Andrew Weil received an A.B. degree cum laude in biology from Harvard College in 1964 and an M.D. degree from Harvard Medical

School in 1968. He served one year with the U.S. Public Health Service at the National Institute of Mental Health in Washington, D.C. He is an extensive traveler and has recently been traveling in South America to collect information on the use of altered states of consciousness by Indian tribes. Regarding alternate consciousness state experiences, he indicates his "belief that the desire to alter consciousness periodically is an innate, normal drive" similar to hunger or the sexual drive. [8]

The conclusions of these men, who are not, as far as I am aware, Christians, are very meaningful and have tremendous spiritual implications. They are saying generally that our Western world view has limited reality to a material-physical construct. We have cut off reality that is other than that. Youth, in a rebellion against the emptiness of that kind of a limited system, have found through drugs other spaces in which to exist. A "trip" is an experience with an aspect of self, free from imprisonment in the very tiny world of the physical and material. They have felt that this exposure to other realities through drugs is meaningful enough to take risks related to one's mental health and even physical life. The problem and the shame are that youth have had to take drugs to be able to have legitimate "other" experiences when one can have an awareness of the experience with these other realities without drugs. Andrew Weil clearly states that drugs, though they have the capacity to trigger highs, do not contain highs. He feels the real danger or risk in using them as the method of altering consciousness is the tendency of the drugs to reinforce an illusory view of cause and effect that makes it harder for the person using them to learn how to maintain highs without dependence on the material world. [9] Carlos Castaneda shows, in his conversations with the Indian medicine man (Don Juan), the difficulty he had breaking out of his traditional categories to believe and experience the mystical world of his instructor (there is some question as to whether the conversations are real or imagined, but the illustration is appropriate either way). It was only by the use of peyote that he could begin to alter his perceptions of reality; and when he did, the drug was no longer necessary. [10]

Some workers in psychic fields are getting people off drugs by helping them to experience other consciousness states without the use of drugs. Many people are learning how to "let their minds go" or how to lead their minds to mysterious and meaningful experiences that are not under traditional Western categories. It is good to remember here what I have previously mentioned as the dangerous possibilities of neurosis, and even psychosis, occurring from irresponsible and premature exploration of alternate consciousness experiences. As Christians, we submit to the leadership of God's Spirit in our spiritual experiences. To go it on your own may be dangerous.

Andrew Weil states strongly and clearly the case for these "other" experiences. He argues that every person is born with an innate drive to experience other states of consciousness at various times; we especially need "to learn how to get away from ordinary egocentered consciousness." He states he believes this drive to be the most important factor in our evolution. He feels nonordinary experiences are vital to us as expressions of our unconscious minds. He also expresses that these nonordinary happenings in the mind serve to integrate the conscious and unconscious, which he believes is the key to life, health, spiritual development, and the fullest use of our nervous systems. He suggests that if we instill fear of these altered states of consciousness in our children, we will force this innate drive underground and that eventually it will show in antisocial ways.[11]

The concept of altered states of consciousness is causing some to think again about traditional psychological definitions. John Lilly indicates changes in his thinking wherein he is beginning to see psychosis as an unusual state of consciousness one has gone into and which has for some reason been interfered with and thus one has become locked up. In his opinion, the essence of psychosis is that someone goes into one of these unusual states and then refuses to come out.[12]

In William James's opinion:

"Our normal waking consciousness, rational consciousness as we call it, is but one special type of consciousness, whilst all about it, parted from it by the filmiest of screens, there lie potential forms of consciousness entirely different."[13]

As telepathy seems to be the experience of everyone, as indicated by Stanley Krippner, so are different states of consciousness.

Meditation

Meditation is a way of altering or controlling one's mental framework. It is learning to use one's mind in a way best for one's physical body. It is learning to discipline one's mind so that in a sense it does not control one but rather one directs it. You are probably aware of the spread of transcendental meditation and other Eastern meditative philosophies in our country. Meditation is really a part of either the biofeedback or alternate consciousness states categories. I personally believe there are many different ways one can effectively draw calmness and strength into one's self. Transcendental meditation is one of them, and it seems effective for many people. There are now an estimated one-quarter million military personnel alone who meditate. Major Carl Simonton, M.D., former chief radiation therapist at Travis Air Force Base, is treating cancer with meditation, along with radiotherapy and self-instruction. I have seen several of his slides showing remarkable cures from cancer in patients who, along with traditional medical treatment, learn to think, or meditate, cancer away.

Robert Ornstein sees meditation as being among the most common and highly perfected of the techniques of traditional psychologies. He indicates that such techniques have been used in almost every culture from ancient Egypt to that of the contemporary Eskimo. He further states that the concept "meditation" refers to techniques that are the product of another type of psychology that aims at personal rather than intellectual knowledge. He sees meditation as a way of "turning down the brilliance of the day, so that everpresent and subtle sources of energy can be perceived within." Meditation is a method to be used in an attempt to separate oneself for a short period from the normal flow of everyday life. It is an attempt to cut down the usual mode of consciousness for the development of a second mode that is also available to humankind.[14]

About this which is available to humankind, Leslie Weatherhead, author of *Psychology, Religion and Healing,* indicates his belief that there are immense energies in the realm of the spirit. He further believes that these can be tapped through prayer and meditation. He thinks that "psychic research . . . will gradually show us how to direct those energies towards the alleviation of our ills."[15]

There are apparently many ways to view meditation and many ways to experience it. Robert Ornstein sees some commonality in all of it, though. He says that one similarity seems to come through all the diverse methods used by different cultures over the years. That single ingredient, in his opinion, is the "attempt to restrict awareness to a single, unchanging source of stimulation for a definite period of time." In the tradition of many this is called "onepointedness of mind."[16]

Meditation has always been a very necessary and meaningful discipline within the Christian faith. Effective Christians find their own "time alone" that adequately supplies them with rich resources for mental and spiritual health. The devotional material available is plentiful for any believer who wishes to use it for growth. Probably two of the best-known daily devotional booklets are *The Upper Room* and *The Secret Place.*

Out of Body

In all likelihood, the most extreme concept of mental phenomena is that called "out of body" experience or "astral projection." A general book to read in this area if you wish a broader understanding is *The Study and Practice of Astral Projection* by Robert Crookal; another is *Journeys Out of the Body* by Robert A. Monroe, a well-known psychic. The body may be like an outer shell with the real person on the inside. Most people would probably not have trouble agreeing with that concept and would think of the inside part as being the personality or the feelings or attitudes of the person. Christians and believers of other religions seem generally to embrace the concept of a soul, but to think of persons being able to move "outside" of their bodies while still alive physically, to experience consciously places other than where they are, leads to a real stretch of imagination for most of us.

A basic theory of out-of-body experience is that a person has two bodily forms. One is a physical form and the other a psychical one. The psychical body would be the spiritual or astral body. Those who espouse this theory feel that under certain conditions, such as sleep, trance, coma, etc., the psychic body may detach itself from the physical body and move around independently. John Lilly has claimed to have had many out-of-body experiences, and he speaks of them freely in *The Center of the Cyclone.*

Many psychics have claimed they have experienced leaving their bodies but only recently have there been laboratory experiments to attest to its occurrence. A man named Ingo Swann claimed to the Stanford Research Institute that he could do this. He was tested in a controlled laboratory setting. Eight of eight times he left his body and correctly identified an object in another room. In the monitoring of his brain waves during the experiment, his alpha waves dropped out when he was out of body. Dr. Stanley Krippner tells of this experiment in an interview for *Psychology Today.*[17] In 2 Corinthians

12:1-4 the apostle Paul talks of a man who was transferred to an experience in another place. In this scripture it seems that Paul did not know if the physical body was there or not.

Thoughtography

Another category is thoughtography or psychic photography. This is the projecting of thought on film. Russian Nelya Mikhailova "can make the letters 'A' or 'O' appear on photo paper. Sometimes she can also transfer a silhouette of a picture she's seen onto photo paper." [18] The most famous person in this category, though, is an American named Ted Serios. He is able to project photographic images onto polaroid film by staring into the lens of a camera with intense concentration. *The World of Ted Serios* by Jule Eisenbud (Paperback Library, 1969) gives an account of his painstaking investigations of psychic photography and the personality of Ted Serios.

Psychic Kinesis

The Russian woman Nelya Mikhailova is absolutely marvelous in the study of psychic kinesis. Psychic kinesis (PK) is mind moving matter. I had lunch with Hugh Lynn Cayce, son of the famous Edgar Cayce. He told me about taking a group of interested researchers into Russia to study their advances in parapsychological phenomena. He related meeting Nelya at a luncheon. She demonstrated to them her abilities: She took the cap of a fountain pen, set it on end, and kind of bounced it across the table and back by intense concentration and some sort of movement of her body. She also took a ring and, in response to her concentration, it slid very quickly across the table and then back into her hand. All who observed were amazed but could not deny it had happened. Ostrander and Schroeder discuss Nelya and her abilities quite thoroughly in *Psychic Discoveries Behind the Iron Curtain.*

Stanford Research Institute has recently tested a young Jewish man, Uri Geller, who reportedly is able to bend and break metal objects by force of will. He has been tested thoroughly. The July, 1973, issue of *Psychic* magazine contains an interesting interview with this controversial and unusual young man. Many of you have probably seen him on talk shows or have read current articles and comments about him.

Psychotronic Generators

We are discovering objects that may be called psychotronic generators or psychic retainers. These objects can store up and give out human energy. A Czechoslovakian named Robert Pavlita has created generators that retain energy and then give it out. They turn small wheels, step up plant growth, purify polluted water, etc. Pavlita stares into the object with concentration and transfers energy.[19]

I heard Douglas Dean the day he returned from the First International Congress of Parapsychology and Psychotronics in Prague. He saw some demonstrations of these phenomena there and said that these motors seem to be charged best by putting them up against the temple of the head. Certain objects seem to store, retain, and carry human energy. Acts 19:11-12 shows some kind of potentially healing phenomena occurring through objects, such as handkerchiefs or aprons. This may be psychotronics in action.

Faith Healing

Another category is faith healing. This is called by parapsychologists "unconventional healing." It includes such things as prayer for the sick, laying on of hands, stroking, new thought healing, magnetic healing, blessing, and other activity that might be classified as spiritual healing. Healing seems to occur for animals and plants as well as people. Here is a partial list of illnesses that seem to respond to faith healing: warts; brain damage; cancer; tumors; scar tissue; diseases of the kidneys, stomach, spleen, liver, and colon; tumors in the lungs, throat, etc.; disorders of the eyes, ears, legs, hips, feet, skin, and nerves; alcoholism and emotional disturbances. The list just mentioned comes from Olga Worrall, Ph.D., who is associate director of the New Life Clinic of the Methodist Church, and is derived from her own known healings.

I heard Olga Worrall when she spoke to the Academy of Parapsychology and Medicine. She gave accounts of some amazing healings stating they could be attested to by reputable physicians. Most of us as Christians probably do believe in healing. There is now, however, unquestionable evidence of the effects of certain aspects of healing which I will discuss later in another chapter where I deal specifically with spiritual healing. You might also read *Faith Healing* by British psychiatrist Louis Rose (Penguin Books, 1971); he attempts to bring the phenomenon of faith healing into line with medical knowledge. What we may find new in our concepts as believers is that there seem to be natural laws operating in healing, and there are many healers, some who do not claim to believe in God. This should not be a problem to believers, for we know that a physician without an active faith can be a healer of physical bodies. A physician once told me that he can only provide the atmosphere for healing, and then the natural healing processes of the body take over. There are also some natural healing processes that occur in aspects of our reality other than the physical, and when the atmosphere or environment is set up, healing occurs. I will discuss this more thoroughly later.

Contact Healing

A specific category of healing is worth mentioning; it is called contact healing. Dr. F. M. Houston's book, *Contact Healing,* demonstrates how this concept is developing into a science; there are places on the body that correspond to the acupuncture points wherein a person can be touched by a high energy person to transfer energy for healing.

The concept of "contact healing" is catching on as a real phenomenon and is being studied as a valid therapeutic procedure to be used for mental as well as physiological treatment. For example, the *National Enquirer* carried the story that America's largest nursing school is now using psychic healing as a part of the healing process and is teaching some students how to do it.

The school is New York University's Division of Nurse Education. Dr. Martha Rogers is the head of the division, and she became aware of the phenomenon from its use and effectiveness on herself. About the phenomenon, she states: "It has remarkable implications for nursing—and I can foresee the time when we'll extend this training to all of our students." [20]

Dr. Dolores Krieger, as associate professor of education, teaches the class on the healing art. Her statement concerning contact healing, or the laying on of hands, follows:

"I think laying on of hands will soon be accepted everywhere as a normal part of hospital routine. There's no limit to what it can cure—arthritis, fever, backache, anything you care to name. It's something that can produce results when all else has failed." [21]

Eyeless Sight

There is another phenomenon called eyeless sight or dermo-optics, bio-introscopy, or paraoptic abilities. A very informative book about this phenomenon is *Psychic Discoveries Behind the Iron Curtain.* In 1962 a Rosa Kuleshova of Russia told her doctor, Iosif M. Goldberg, that she could see with her fingers. He blindfolded her and she moved the fingers of her right hand over sheets of paper, naming colors. He put books, magazines, newspapers in front of her, and her fingers read as easily as her eyes.

Goldberg, a neuropathologist, tested and retested her and finally took Rosa to a regional conference of the Society of Psychologists which met in Nizhniy Tagil in the fall of 1962. She amazed those attending. The Biophysics Institute of the Soviet Academy of Sciences in Moscow invited her to come in for experiments in their laboratories. After a period of daily experiments, M. S. Smirnov, spokesman for the institute, said: "Rosa Kuleshova can read a text by touching it, she can identify colors and light with her hands."[22]

In 1964 Bob Brigham of *Life* magazine visited Rosa at the Moscow clinic. She did things such as reading his business card with her elbow. Some think that the whole body can possibly be taught to "see." This has tremendous implications for the physically blind.[23]

Acupuncture

Most of us have heard of acupuncture by now. Many people, both professional and nonprofessional, accept acupuncture and say it works. There is much testimonial attestation by doctors, dentists, scientifically controlled experiments, and reports. Acupuncture has become a definite medical tool to many, and others who do not use it consider it valid and accepted. It consists of inserting needles in various parts of the body to produce various kinds of effects. It is specifically associated with a philosophy of human nature, and many who practice it in this country also find it important to teach the Oriental philosophy behind acupuncture, too. I will discuss the philosophy later.

The September, 1973, issue of *Intellectual Digest* states:

> ... although critics call acupuncture everything from fad to autohypnosis, there is no longer any doubt that it works. It makes surgery possible without any chemical anesthetic. It reduces or eliminates the symptoms of a variety of illnesses. Preliminary surveys by the National Institutes of Health show that of some 500 American patients treated with acupuncture for chronic pain, about two out of three were helped.

Acupuncture research projects are already planned and underway at at least 25 medical schools and universities in the U.S.[24]

"Dr. Jane F. Lee, physician and researcher in acupuncture at the University of California Medical Center, told the California Dental Association all a dentist needs to do is puncture with a silver needle a spot on the hand between thumb and forefinger . . . then drill away or yank away the molar."[25] Some individuals appear overoptimistic about the eventual overall use. Dr. Ronald Katz, who heads the anesthesiology department at UCLA, predicts that the role of acupuncture in American medicine will be similar to that of hypnosis—used primarily when drugs are impractical. Acupuncture, however, seems to be here to stay.

Astrology

Astrology has captured the attention of countless numbers of people. It teaches that the planets have an influence on a child at birth and this establishes a pattern of influences that allows for a fairly consistent system for understanding the personality. Many newspapers and magazines, radios, and other forms of media carry information about one's horoscope wherein some form of understanding of the future can be realized from an observation of the planets and stars. We know that the planets affect the tides of the earth and the surface tides on the sun. It is highly likely that there is energy magnetism from the planets that plays on the energy of our bodies also. The influences are not controlling but they are real. Dr. Eugen Jonas, director of the Astra Center of Czechoslovakia, has developed what he calls "Astrological Birth Control." It involves the relationship between the sun and moon at each woman's birth. He claims to be able to determine for a couple when pregnancy must occur to have a girl or a boy.[26]

The universe seems to be in an extremely consistent order, and thus, if we knew more about a number of things, we could possibly determine patterns of consistency that could be very accurate in each aspect of our ordered universe—patterns that would show clear indication of a number of life tendencies in all living species. This consistency may explain why people who study the shape of the head, hands, feet, etc., can sometimes amaze us by seemingly unusual awareness of a personality by observation of that particular part of the body. This could account for phenomena such as palm reading and character reading by analysis of handwriting. I remember a girl in one of the groups I was leading who could determine what a person's feet looked like from seeing the person and the personality. She could also come amazingly close to guessing a person's looks (general features) and personality from observing his or her feet. We did an experiment; we showed her only a person's feet and she guessed what the person looked like and what the personality was like.

This may serve as an example of what I meant when I said that there is seemingly a consistency in all things, and, if information were available in detail, each thing we call individual might be found to have a clear pattern within itself that could convey a picture of the "whole." If it is true with hands, feet, etc., it is most likely much more strongly noticed and verified in very large bodies, such as the planets and the stars. In the "parts" you can recognize the "whole," and in the "whole" you can recognize the "parts."

Plant Life

Much of our awareness of the unity and oneness of all things is coming from our study of plants. It has been discovered, for example, that hours before it rains, the stem and leaves of a plant are unusually active. A plant seems to know rain is coming. The Russians are learning how to use this information for weather prediction.[27]

Researchers are able to connect plants to sensing devices to determine how they react to certain occurrences. There are two experiments I am aware of that were shown on television. One was the burning of a plant. Sensing devices were attached to another plant in the same room. The plant with the sensing devices felt and reacted to the burning of the other plant.

In the other experiment, a plant was burned by a particular man. Different people came into the room one at a time after this, and when the individual who had burned the plant came in, definite reactions were picked up from the plant. It actually seemed to know who burned it. Plants appear to be sensitive to thoughts and attitudes and can apparently tell if someone doesn't like them. Cleve Backster, of the Backster Research Foundation of New York City, is one who has done much experimentation with plants, such as the burning of one and observing the reaction in another, also observing the reaction of a plant to the death of a shrimp.

The phenomena I have discussed here are just some of the data that are nudging many to rethink their view of the universe. I have not dealt with many other areas where information is available. I have attempted to give just a partial picture that will acquaint the reader with a wider view of parapsychological categories.

As you contemplate this chapter, you may find it interesting to explore the different personal experiences you may have had with happenings which seemed unnatural to you. Many people are hesitant to do so because of feeling different as a result of these experiences. Are some of the occurrences mentioned in this chapter easier to accept than others? If so, which ones, and why? Would your concern for a person change if your awareness of that person's problems came from ESP, or from God's Spirit, or is there no difference? Do any of the areas being researched make you feel uneasy inside? Do you feel threatened or nervous about any of them? If so, can you point out what is causing those feelings? If you sensed something as a "strong feeling inside," would you pay attention to it? Where does that strong feeling come from?

Chapter III

PHOTOGRAPHING
ANOTHER BODY

Kirlian Photography

Over twenty-five years ago Dr. Semyon Kirlian and his wife, Valentina, accidentally discovered, while working on another project, an amazing photographic process wherein they could record on film a luminous energy coming from the human body. This luminous energy has been claimed to have been seen by certain "unusual" people throughout history. This is possibly the visualized phenomenon that was the origin of the halo on saints, angels, Jesus, and other charismatic religious leaders all over the world.

This mode of photography is now known variously as Kirlian radiation, or simply spark photography. It is also called "electrography" by some. This photographic process works by passing a spark of electricity through an object that is lying in close proximity to film. The picture is obtained without camera or lens. If you wish to experiment with this process (there are a number of "garage" researchers who have made significant contributions), place the object to be photographed on film between two metal objects and apply voltage. If you are photographing pictures of a portion of the human body, only one electrode is needed since the body acts as a ground. (You can use a tesla coil to multiply the voltage and frequency on the electrical field.) When the current is activated in a darkened room, rays of light are seen issuing from the object's edges. The light is recorded on film.

The emanations showing through this process are called "bioplasma," "electron emission," "corona discharge," "energy body," "astrobody," or "life field." Every living thing—humans, animals, plants—apparently has a material body *and* an energy body. This is the aura, a radiating, luminous cloud, surrounding the body that for centuries some gifted people apparently have been able to see.

An Energy Body

Dr. Thelma Moss is assistant professor in residence at the Neuropsychiatric Institute at UCLA in Los Angeles. Her area is medical psychology. She visited the laboratory of Dr. V. I. Inyushen at Kazakh University, USSR. There, movies of Kirlian photography were shown her, and she affirms that "there is an energy body that is a duplicate of the physical body but made of a finer substance, invisible under ordinary circumstances." [1]

This energy body is thought to be the main body. The physical body somehow mirrors what is happening in the energy body. When Dr. Douglas Dean first saw movies of this phenomenon in Russia, he was amazed. He states:

> I gasped in astonishment when I was shown the spectacular films made by the Russians. . . . There was the human aura, as the psychics have described it, before my eyes—flowing from the body of the subject, in wave after wave of vivid color.
>
> It emanated especially from the areas of the back and neck. I gazed fascinatedly as color succeeded color in the aura, each with its own significance as to the state of mind and body of the subject. [2]

All living things—plants, animals, and people—are encased in an envelope of energy. This energy "skin" may protect us from the outside energy elements like our physical skin protects us in our physical world. It may also allow for the inner energy life of the individual to exist in a "self" composition as the skin encloses the physical self of the person.

This energy body is ever pulsating and moving. It seems to circulate continuously through the human body. Illness, emotion, state of mind, thoughts, and fatigue all seem to make their distinct impression and imprint on the pattern of energy flow and on the color of its emissions. This energy body is a whole unified system or organism in itself. There is a seemingly strict ratio between the physical body and the energy body—between the atomic-molecular matter and the plasmic state of living things.

The ancient Chinese have long taught that one is not a machinelike collection of parts, but a powerhouse of unusual energy. This is called "life force" or "vital energy." Such energy appears to be the substance that fills the universe, and thus everyone is linked to all other living things.

All living beings apparently have not only a physical body comprised of atoms and molecules but also a counterpart body made up of an energy, or electrical phenomenon, or something we cannot yet accurately describe, but we can see it and observe it now; it is not like anything we have previously known.

Could it be that this is what we call the Spirit? In Genesis, the creation story of man describes man's created body, and then God breathed into that body and it became a living soul. God breathed into that body life energy, and the body sparked alive. This may be the Spirit of God that, according to the Scripture, exists everywhere and is the life of all things. Theologians will probably be searching the Scriptures in new ways in days ahead.

The different colors of the aura and the amount of energy radiating from the subject can show the state the subject is in as to health or illness. Russian physicians are already using Kirlian photography to determine treatment. This energy can be obstructed, and this creates an environment for disease and can cause illness. (This is where acupuncture philosophy fits in. We will discuss this aspect a little later.) It can be passed from one person to another and from a person to an object, and vice versa. This will also be discussed in greater detail when we deal with faith healing.

It is observed that when a hole is torn in a leaf, the material leaf has a hole but the energy body is still there—as at death it was still present. We have all heard stories about people with missing arms or legs still "feeling" them after they were gone. Dr. Douglas Dean believes the Russians have "phantom photos" of missing human limbs.[3] This is most likely what is occurring in the phenomenon of "phantom limbs" referred to by psychologists. With pictures showing the energy part still present, it seems to be more than just nerve endings. After a period of time the energy limb seems to be absorbed into the rest of the body.

This bioplasm body has been photographed while leaving the

body, like a lifting mist, after death. Some psychics have spoken of observing this phenomenon. Eileen Garrett, president of the Parapsychology Foundation of New York, for example, says she sees spirals of energy leaving the bodies of the recently dead up to three days after death.

This is an interesting discovery, and it may be that Christians, or other believers in life after death, may have sound scientific proof that when the body dies, that which was the person, inside or alongside of that physical housing, goes on. If this proves to be the case, one will not need faith to believe in life after death, but faith as trusting God in the experience of life through death to life will still be as real and relevant as ever. Dr. Dean, in his report from the First International Congress of Parapsychology and Psychotronics, says that they are reaffirming continually the existence of this bioplasma or energy body.

The Mind and the Energy Body

The basic influence, or effecting factor, on this life energy seems to be our thoughts, our minds. Our minds can direct it, affect its color, and thus create illness or health. No wonder Jesus said so much about our thought life. (In the last chapter there is a more complete discussion of the mind.) Our thoughts occur, in my opinion, in this energy body that some are saying seems to be the primary body. This energy body has a physical body for its existence in this physical-material world. The brain may be just the "mechanical" device by which the body is operated. When the body is not needed, the mind seems to be able to function aside from the brain. The mind and our bioplasma bodies may just use the physical body. The brain seems to be the fantastic control center for all the functionings of the physical body. Death is like an evacuation from a physical body no longer needed, no longer wanted, or no longer able to function. All the physiological parts, including the brain, are left behind. The pulsating energy body may therefore be the electrical charge bringing each physical cell and each particle to life.

The discovery of the energy body has allowed us a framework for understanding a great deal about parapsychological phenomena. As our physical bodies live by an interchange with the surroundings around us, so our energy bodies apparently live by an interchange with the energy around us. We live physically by drawing air, food, water, etc., from our environment, and we participate in the interchange by working to discover and produce some of the resources necessary for existence. This is seemingly true also of our energy lives. We are apparently continually drawing life energy from all around us into our living and are also giving it out for the living of others. This interchange seems also to occur between plants and animals, animals and animals, and plants and plants.

Faith Healing

There are life interchanges that are conscious. These we do intentionally and our awareness of what we can do purposefully is expanding immensely. Healing is one of the categories of conscious interchange being understood and recognized by medicine and science due to the discovery of the bioplasma or energy body. One can photograph a before and after healing. When one can empirically show a major difference in the energy body of a person or thing after being touched by a "healer," the fact of a literal transference of life energy (whatever it is) must be accepted.

Healing seems to occur basically through this transfer of energy from a highly energized person to an ill person whose energy is low. Faith healers have an ability to give to someone or something else their energy, or, through them, energy goes to the other. I will mention a few of several researchers studying the effects of the "laying on of hands." Most of us are probably more familiar with the biblical practice of laying on of hands than with other phenomena mentioned. We may be in the process of understanding what it has meant as a very literal occurrence of a very real happening, and not just a symbolism.

Dr. Bernard Grad is a research assistant in the gerontological unit of the Allan Memorial Institute of Psychiatry at McGill University in Montreal, Quebec. He has been studying the effects of "laying on of hands" on plants, animals, and human subjects. He relates that it is obvious that those exposed to the laying on of hands heal faster. He also points out, by the way, that one can draw energy away from something. This inhibits growth and health. A low energy person can draw energy from other persons. This may be someone who always depresses people when they are around that person.[4]

Thelma S. Moss, of UCLA, has done a great deal of research with photographic evidence of healing energy on plants and animals. She gave an extensive report at the Dimensions of Healing Symposium sponsored by the Academy of Parapsychology and Medicine at

Stanford University in 1972, September 30 to October 3. She showed slides of leaves in various conditions and the effects of healers on the auras of those leaves.[5]

In the July 30, 1972, issue of the *Los Angeles Times* there are pictures of leaves and fingerprints showing before and after conditions of energy states. There is the picture of a healer's fingerprint, healthy and glowing. Next is the picture of the patient, a very weak and dulled energy image. Next is the fingerprint of the patient, after being the recipient of the healer's treatment. It is the brightest picture or the healthiest corona of them all. The last picture is one of the fingerprint of the healer after healing the patient; it definitely shows a loss of energy that apparently occurred from the transfer of energy for the healing. It seems to take just a short time, however, for the healer to "build up" again.

Certain aspects of faith healing appear to occur from this transfer of energy, and it is accepted by many and is being accepted by more people. Dr. Krieger, of New York University's Division of Nurse Education, says, in relation to the healing she does: "Once I've found the area where the trouble lies, I lay my hands on the patient for between 5 and 20 minutes. I think consciously all the time about transferring energy from my body to the patient's."[6]

Olga Worrall told the audience at the 1973 annual Symposium of the Academy of Parapsychology and Medicine that many hospitals were beginning to use faith healers in conjunction with "conventional" healing. I have already mentioned one, the Division of Nurse Education at New York University. We indeed live in a new day.

Jesus and Healing

A lot of the healing Jesus performed seemed to result from a transfer of some kind of force, power, energy, or life substance. Mark gives the account of the woman with the blood disease who slipped through the crowds to touch Jesus' garment. In verse 30 of chapter 5, Mark reports, "And Jesus, perceiving in himself that power had gone forth from him, immediately turned about in the crowd, and said, 'Who touched my garments?'"

This seems to be the general phenomenon occurring in Jesus' healings. Luke 6:19 says, "and all the crowd sought to touch him, for power came forth from him and healed them all." This power or energy, or whatever it was from Christ, created health; it removed illness, disease, and seemingly all disfunctioning.

The crowds knew that this "pulling of power" from Jesus was efficacious, for they seemed continually to bring the ill to touch him. Matthew 14:35-36 says:

> And when the men of that place recognized him, they sent round to all that region and brought to him all that were sick, and besought him that they might only touch the fringe of his garment; and as many as touched it were made well.

And in Mark 3:10 we read "For he had healed many, so that all who had diseases pressed upon him to touch him."

To touch Jesus is to experience healing power flowing through the body, correcting everything in its path, or adjusting every incongruency in the body that it might work in real harmony, which is health.

The book of Acts shows some Christians radiating with energy and thus actively involved in healing. Peter was one of these. Acts 5:14-16 says:

> And more than ever believers were added to the Lord, multitudes both of men and women, so that they even carried out the sick into the streets, and laid them on beds and pallets, that as Peter came by at least his shadow might fall on some of them. The people also gathered from the towns around Jerusalem, bringing the sick and those afflicted with unclean spirits, and they were all healed.

The apostle Paul was another healer. Acts 19:11-12 states:

> And God did extraordinary miracles by the hands of Paul, so that handkerchiefs or aprons were carried away from his body to the sick, and diseases left them and the evil spirits came out of them.

The healing power was carried through objects; this was indicated on page 39 in relation to psychotronic generators. When James encourages the elders (James 5) to pray for the sick and to anoint them, it may be within the context of a group of highly energized spiritual men who were instruments for the transfer of healing power to the ill person. Christians should be a highly energized group of people giving God's life energy or power to life around them.

Romans 12:6-8, which speaks of the different gifts people have been given, has a natural flavor to me. That is, I think God looks at our personalities and grants gifts that fit into our natural abilities, but he also expands or augments these abilities. The Holy Spirit brings us to our fullest potential if we allow it to occur. For example, Peter and Paul already had natural leadership abilities. Jesus shows us the potential of a whole person—one who is one with God, himself/herself, and the world around him/her. Everything Jesus did is within our potential. In fact, Jesus said that we would do even greater things. Many of what we call parapsychological occurrences can be seen in Jesus, from clairvoyance—such as seeing Nathanael before Philip brought Nathanael to Jesus (John 1:45-47)—to prognostications of the future, which are abundant in the Gospels. An example might be Jesus' prediction of the destruction of Jerusalem which occurred in 70 A.D.

When we open ourselves up to God, God may bring alive an aspect of our reality or ability to an unusually full degree, often taking an ability to proportions that amaze us and making it appear miraculous. For example, healers may simply be high energy people. Some persons are suggesting that we need to go on a search for healers. This could be done with the use of the special photographic processes that reveal the bioplasma body. People with very alive coronas can be taught to transfer their energy to others. There are healers who do not believe in God; purely because they are highly energized, they can transfer this vital force to others, causing healing to occur. If such a person could let God augment that ability, he or she might be able to help to a higher extent.

Building One's Energy

I wish to mention that if we desire to reach our finest potential, it will entail learning how to draw life energy unto ourselves, as well as learning how to give it to others. God's Spirit is all around us, his vital force is in the air and animates all that exists. We must learn how to allow God's Spirit to be a part of us as Jesus did.

The Gospels show Jesus often getting up much earlier than the others to be by himself, or "getting lost" from the crowds, apparently to "renew" himself. Here are some verses that emphasize or point out this aspect of Jesus' living: Mark 1:35: "And in the morning, a great while before day, he rose and went out to a lonely place, and there he prayed." Matthew 14:23: "He went up on the mountain by himself to pray. When evening came, he was there alone." Luke 4:42: "And when it was day he departed and went into a lonely place." Luke 6:12: "In these days he went out to the mountain to pray; and all night he continued in prayer to God." Luke 5:16: "But he withdrew to the wilderness and prayed."

There are several other places, too, but the verses mentioned will be adequate as examples of the importance Jesus placed on being by himself for his own "building up." Every person needs to learn how to build up his/her own resources. If one does not successfully find his/her life vital and fulfilling from his/her learning to draw from God and the resources God has abundantly distributed all around us, he/she may be drawing too much from others. Jesus told the woman at the well that he would put "within" her a spring of life's water welling up to eternal life. This water, in my thinking, is the vital life force of God's Spirit. How marvelous it is to have it pouring forth into one's life from the abundance of God and his universe!

Acupuncture

The revelation of energy bodies and the fact of the transference of this energy also explain categories other than faith healing. Take acupuncture, for example. Traditionally, acupuncture is a philosophy in itself. It says that human beings are in the center of the universe. There are two opposing forces struggling or interplaying within their bodies. The task is to keep these two forces in balance or disease will occur. The two forces are symbolized as the yin and the yang. They might be understood as the forces of night and day, male and female, cold and hot, negative and positive, or active and passive. These forces are opposites, but are a unity.

Health occurs from the free flow of the life force called "chi." Illness occurs from an imbalance between the forces yin and yang, which causes obstructions in the flow of chi. Health is restored by creating a balance again.

The body has theoretical lines of orientation or direction through which the chi flows. There are what might be seen as channels, called "meridians." Meridians are like tunnels through which the chi flows. There are about seventy meridians. Some think the flow of energy through the body is in the pattern of a figure eight.

Acupuncture is the sticking of needles into certain areas and turning them, which activates or expedites the flow of energy in the part of the body that has become obstructed. It creates the proper balance again in the system and causes health. Health is the condition present with the normal flow of this life force through the human body. This theory of acupuncture has a known history of at least three thousand years and probably five thousand.

I mentioned previously that the contact points of touch or contact healing coincide with the acupuncture points of healing. There are photographs of "before and after" acupuncture treatment that show differences in the aura or corona equal to that noticed in faith healing.

Energy and Other Phenomena

Related to telepathy, Douglas Dean has stated that the Russians have taken pictures of the lines of energy going between two people who were in telepathic communication with each other.[7] Thought apparently can be transferred within this energy and with concentration can be sent to another person, or this energy may be a particular form of thought.

Thoughtography may be one's energy leaving a thought picture on film. Psychic kinesis may be this life force concentrated enough to move or influence matter. Psychotron motors simply retain this now visible energy and dole it out as it is used.

The fact of an energy body seems to be very sure and possibly, as mentioned previously, is the primary body. It has direct effects on the physical body, and the physical body can affect it. Our spirits are not our physical bodies; for when one dies, the life of the physical body ends but the "person" lives on. Whether this energy body is the primary reality of our eternal existence will be left to further research by scientists and theologians.

One can talk about souls and spirits of persons and find a lot of support from many parapsychological researchers. The terminology may be different, but the fact of a continuing living is being more accepted and thus is becoming important to many more people. J. B. Rhine comments:

> Any sort of survival of any portion of the personality, for any length of time, holds such significance for human thinking and feeling as to dwarf almost all other scientific discovery by comparison.[8]

As you think about this chapter, you might wish to consider whether you are a high- or low-energy person. Is it difficult for you to think of energy being transferred from one human to another? Does the concept of healing as suggested take away from the gospel, or does it possibly even add to its impact? Is it easier for us to understand what prayer for the sick might mean within this perspective? Do you believe that persons have the potential of Jesus? What understanding do you have of your own "life energy"? How do you build it or refresh it every day? Have you thought that you might literally be able to give part of your life to someone else? If your were sick, would you call in people to touch you and pray for you as James suggests? If so, what would you expect to happen?

Chapter IV

ANGELS
AND DEMONS

In this chapter, I am going to discuss occurrences that seem to involve "outside" entities. To be aware of "outside" entities and to be able to benefit from our awareness may be profoundly important in the future. There are certain aspects or categories of parapsychological phenomena that seem to be explained by the activity of "beings" that are not a part of our physical-material world. I mean they are not a visible part, having a physical form as we do.

I use the word "entity" because it bypasses the need for other definitive information. That is, an entity is an experiencing life that has a character of independence within itself. It can say "I am." The term "entity," which is used freely by parapsychologists, can then refer to persons, to other intelligent life, to angels, to demons, even to God. The word "being" or the concept of other beings might be analogous to the definition of entity.

The Bible shows us the participation of countless numbers of beings that are not in a physical form like ours—at least not usually—and which are involved in the affairs of human beings. Psychics have always seemed to believe this, and now parapsychologists are beginning to give it serious thought and consideration. In fact, the current publicity given to demon possession and obsession has brought to life the concept of exorcism, casting out or getting rid of evil or negative entities.

Many Christians believe in other entities, that they are existent and that they are involved in our affairs. We don't, however, always understand practically what this means in everyday life. That is, we seem to have a theoretical framework that allows for a conceptualization of "angels and demons" but don't have an understanding of what it means in our living.

For example, should we look for "angels" around us? Should we seek to communicate with them, to learn from them? The Bible shows them clearly involved in life in the leading and directing of God. Some people think that because we have the Holy Spirit, God is not using "angels" in a visual and overt way as he did previously. However, after the Holy Spirit was in the believers, after Pentecost, after one could be led from the "inside," God still showed angels appearing in a physical-material form to be a part of his working. Examples are: the one who brought Peter out of prison, as shown in Acts 12:6-8, and the one who joined the apostle Paul in the bottom of a storm-tossed ship to tell him God was going to save him and all others on board if they would follow His instructions (Acts 27:21-25).

Psychics and Other Beings

Some people today are claiming they are contacting and being contacted by entities who are not in our physical-material form. Are they? If they are, who is it they are contacting or by whom are they being contacted?

The first person I encountered who claimed to have had communication from that which was "outside" of himself was Edgar Cayce. My encounter with him was through his books and through his son Hugh Lynn Cayce, whom I have met and with whom I have conversed. The classic biography of Edgar Cayce's life, *There Is a River,* was written by Thomas Sugrue.

Edgar Cayce was a very dedicated Christian. He read the Bible through every year from the time he was a young man. He attended church regularly and taught a Sunday school class most of his life. He sought to understand everything in light of the Scriptures and the Christian life. His gift involved going into a trance, and while in the trance he seemed to be able to tap into another resource of knowledge and information. One could ask him questions, and he could answer almost anything. The person (or entity) speaking through him could diagnose illnesses and disease and could give suggestions for treatment and cure. This phenomenon seemed to occur either from Edgar Cayce's own unconscious or from an outside being speaking through him. I feel it is the latter, due to the amount of information given, the nature of the information, and the apparent freedom from time and space shown in the diagnosis.

Much has occurred for the benefit of humankind from this mysterious life. From 1901 until shortly before his death in 1944, Edgar Cayce entered into his sleep-like trance at least 16,000 times, and from him during this time have come thousands of bits of information to help people in their living. His son Hugh Lynn continues to run an organization called "The Association for Research and Enlightenment."

My encounter with Edgar Cayce motivated me to consider opening up to new possible categories of reality. I did not agree with everything said through him, but the fact that the phenomena were occurring awakened in me an interest in understanding how it was happening and what it meant. I want also to share a couple of other personal experiences I have had with men who attribute their gifts to "outside" entity involvement, for the purpose of demonstrating some of the occurrences that made it seem necessary to me to develop a philosophy of my own for understanding the phenomena. I will also mention some other phenomena occurring that can be attributed to outside beings. Again, I want to reiterate that I am not trying to persuade or convince anyone of the validity of the examples, but rather to demonstrate the types of things occurring that give rise to serious examination and research.

In Phoenix, Arizona, my brother took my wife and me to see a man called "The Phoenix Oracle." His name is Richard Ireland, and he was demonstrating his psychic powers to a fairly large audience. He called a couple of skeptics up and had them put tape over his eyes, then a blindfold, then more tape. Tape was even put over his nose. He definitely could not see, and even if he could, the room was too dark to make clear visual experience a reality. He then proceeded to name serial numbers on different dollar bills without even looking at them. He read notes and answered questions with seeming accuracy. My brother and I tore a $10 bill in half and told him if he could point to where we were sitting and give the serial number accurately, we would give him the other half. Needless to say, he did.

The next day we saw him in another setting where he did some discussing of his gift and more answering of questions from people who were wondering about the future. He stated that he heard voices from entities that spoke to his mind and they would answer these questions. My wife asked him about a job. She had just graduated from school with her master's degree, hoping to teach, and it was during the time when teachers were in overabundance. She had looked everywhere in our area, and nothing was open. He told her not to wonder anymore, that when we got back from our vacation, a job would come to her. It did just that, the very week we returned. This may have been coincidence, but the timing caused us to wonder.

The Psychic World of Peter Hurkos by Norma Lee Browning is an interesting book in the area of psychics. It is full of illustrations of the phenomena called "postgnostication" and "prognostication." Postgnostication refers to seeing the past, and prognostication refers to seeing the future. A couple of examples of the former are Peter Hurkos's telling a woman the actual date on her birth certificate when the woman herself did not know, and his telling, from holding an object, what had happened in the past to a certain person. Hurkos has been used by the police in the solving of a number of criminal cases. He has, reportedly, been very successful. An example of prognostication was his prediction to Norma, the author of the book, in February that they would not be selling their house (it was going up for sale) until August, that they would lose money, and that the buyers would live with them for a short time before their moving. It all happened. Peter Hurkos said to Norma later: "I tell only what I see and hear, what the voice tells me." [1] He must have felt the voice was from some outside being.

I have not mentioned previously the phenomenon called "psychic surgery" because it is extremely controversial. However, I think it might be important just to touch on the subject since it includes the alleged involvement of "outside" entities. About fifty people a week, from all over the country, fly to the Philippines to see a psychic surgeon operate. [2] This man is Antonio Agpaoa—called Dr. Tony— who is in his middle thirties and has a fourth-grade education. He is a psychic surgeon and operates by making an incision in the flesh with his bare hands and removing with his fingers "what is not supposed to be there." He then closes the flesh with no trace of a scar. Patients can take movies, and there are at least four sets of films circulating in the Bay Area of Northern California. Dr. William A. Nolen, an M.D., has extensively proven a lot of fakery in this area of psychic activity, and he reveals this in his book *Healing,* published in 1974 by Random House. However, many doctors are visiting the Philippines and other countries where operations of this nature are taking place, and they are finding some evidence on some occasions of genuine phenomena. Harold Sherman, one of our foremost sensitives and writers in the area of psychic phenomena, states:

> Some doctors have analyzed blood samples and tissue before and after operations, to substantiate their genuineness, and I have seen affidavits signed by ten doctors and surgeons testifying that the operations they observed were genuine.[3]

Andrija Puharich is an M.D. He formerly was Senior Research Scientist at the New York University Medical Center. He is now doing free-lance research on parapsychology. When I heard him speak at the Academy of Parapsychology and Medicine convention in 1973, he reported on his observations of psychic surgery. One of the statements he made, and this is why I include psychic surgery in this part of our study, was that there were guides, which the surgeons took as deceased persons, probably doctors, who were telling them what to do and how to do it.

I was interested in a newspaper article in the *San Francisco Chronicle* about Rosemary Brown of London. The article stated that she has written a whole musical library herself. She claims, though, that every note has been "dictated" to her by the great musicians, such as Bach, Liszt, and Chopin. She says that she met Liszt in a vision when she was seven years old, and at that time he told her she would be continuing to compose music for the masters. It is said in the article that, if she is not being dictated to, she is one of the most remarkable composer-musicians of our time. The possibility has been entertained that this phenomenon might explain the child prodigy.

Merced College invited Russ Burgess, a psychic, to come and put on an assembly for the students. I know the Dean of Student Activities very well and am aware of the things, through him, that occurred prior to Russ Burgess's coming. I also attended the assembly and observed his program. The week before Mr. Burgess arrived, he mailed a sealed envelope containing two slips of paper— one with the headlines of the newspaper the day he would be here and the other with a set of digits. During the program the student body president opened the envelope that had been received a week earlier. The headlines were almost verbatim to those of the *San Francisco Chronical* that day. Russ Burgess then went into the audience and had three different people put down three digits each. A fourth person added them up and the total was the number he had sent a week earlier.

I took Mr. Burgess out to lunch and discussed the program with him. His prognostications come to him through what is called "psychic" or "automatic" writing. Psychic writing is a concept of letting your hand be "taken over." Someone else writes through you, or types through you, as you let your hands be led on the typewriter. Ruth Montgomery states that *A World Beyond* was written as the world-famous psychic Arthur Ford, who was dead at the time, typed through her.[4]

The examples I have given here offer you a picture of a phenomenon occurring that, if it really is occurring, seems to be attributed to and explained by other entity involvement. It seems to be happening; so, what does it say and what does it mean to Christians? Other entities seem to many to be interacting with us, whether on a level as unsophisticated as the Ouija board or as sophisticated as the concept of angels being here to show us God's will. I should add here that most of the material on Ouija boards which I have read has been negative with regard to their use. Apparently it has led to many negative experiences for too many people.

There are many people involved in other entity belief frameworks that would include categories traditionally thought to be in the occult area: witchcraft, black and white; ghosts; the living dead; apparitions, talking with the dead; and others.

Prognostications and Time

Prognostications are causing some researchers to do a great deal of thinking about what "time" is. Opinions about prognostications spread from thinking about awarenesses of the future being foreknowledge by outside entities' analyses of occurrences that are in the process of becoming—or in the actual course of realization—to thinking that there is nothing but the present. Some researchers are suggesting that time does not even exist, that there is just the sequencing of single events that are overlapping. Maybe there is nothing but the present, which is all that is, in interaction with all that is, all the time.

Richard Neff suggests that time may be an illusion in human experience. He feels that events which we experience in our world may be affected by minds which exist on a plane different from the plane on which our human minds exist. He also feels that it may be possible that the human can pick up enough by ESP to evaluate the material subconsciously and be able to predict accurately what will happen. Neff entertains the possibility that events which we view in a certain time sequence may not be seen that way from another plane.[5]

In Robert Ornstein's view, there is a difference between a linear mode and a nonlinear mode. In the linear mode time is directional wherein we are carried from the past into the future. The present is always moving back behind us, therefore. In the nonlinear mode though, only the present exists. For us an event is considered "paranormal" if it does not fit into or within the coordinates of the linear mode we are used to.[6]

It seems to me that prognostications would logically involve either the controlling of the variables effecting that certain outcome, or knowing the outcome ahead. To know the outcome ahead would mean that in some sense it already had happened. It may be that from observing the behavior of humankind, and particularly individuals, there is a fairly clear and noticeable pattern that would allow for a high reliability factor of predictability. Humankind, by observation from the "outside," may be fairly easy to figure out.

The "misses" of psychics may possibly relate to "unexpected" decisions or choices people make that throw a wrench into normally high predictability. We confuse the outside entities. I believe life is basically "laid out" to a degree beyond that with which most people would feel comfortable, and we are on this "laid out" plan that will occur that way unless we consciously and intentionally change it.

God has laid out the movements of history to achieve his plans and purposes. This is what I think of as predestination. However, I think that each person participates in the planning of his or her own life either by consciously being aware of joining God in its formation or by thinking his or her own motives and intentions are creating sequencing events that lay it out for him or her. Whatever one's conceptions of time are, or one's understanding of his or her choices, there is apparently a high probability that it is fairly well seen ahead, and thus events are highly predictable.

We seem to be both individual and inescapably part of the whole universe. We may not be able to evade or ignore a certain amount of high predictability about ourselves because we are part of a well-ordered system. The more we discover about ourselves, the more we may see universal patterns in ourselves. At the same time, however, there seems to be an individuality about us that is uniquely "our own." Our uniqueness does not seem to be in areas where universal patterns are seen, such as physical characteristics and general personality patterns, but rather in the subjective aspect of ourselves, such as our hopes, dreams, visions, loves, perspectives, and commitments.

We are paradoxes. Our actions are highly predictable in that we are inescapably a part of the universe wherein we fit into its movement as a whole. But, at the same time, we are uniquely individual wherein we are actually on our own journey. No one is exactly like us in this aspect of ourselves where we seem to chart our own course. Our job seems to be to become more submissive to the universal patterns of God's universe, *and,* at the same time, to become more and more individual in the uniqueness of our own journey.

Predictions from psychics that are amazingly accurate at times may be explained by the outside entities' awareness and understanding of these universal patterns. A great deal about us is probably controlled by these universal factors, and thus can be accurately foretold. The less one uses the potential creativity of one's own individuality, the more predictable one seems to be. The more one is individual—willing to risk, chance, try the new—the less one will probably be predictable. The task is to be the distinct person God wants one to be—and that most likely won't be exactly like anyone else—and to be one's part of the whole.

When one is born, all the realities of heredity are present as the progenitors leave their "marks" on their offspring. Physiological characteristics are fairly well determined. All the "energy" realities are also present, though, from everywhere—which include the position of the planets, stars, etc. These energy forces apparently determine certain energy characteristics as they interplay with the bioplasma body and seem to influence certain personality tendencies. Certain outside entities are apparently aware of all these factors and from them make accurate predictions.

Angels

The Bible says a lot about "outside" influences. These influences come under the division or designation of "angels" or "demons." I am not attempting to do a thorough report of either angelology or demonology. I wish simply to show how readily the Scriptures seem to understand and teach a constant involvement with our world of entities that are not an immediate part of our physical-material world.

In Hebrews 1:14 we see angels pictured as ministering spirits sent forth from God to serve, for the sake of those who are to obtain salvation. There are apparently countless numbers of them. When Jesus was taken from Gethsemane, he reminded his disciples that at his appeal his Father would have sent more than twelve legions of angels. A legion was comprised of three thousand to six thousand foot soldiers and one hundred to seven hundred mounted soldiers. The maximum would mean 80,400 angels (Matthew 26:53).

Angels apparently do exist and there are myriads of them. They are helping to bring in the kingdom of heaven, and they are available to God's people when they need help. Psalm 91:11 says, "For he will give his angels charge of you, to guard you in all your ways." They are all around us and apparently appear when they are needed. When they do appear, they seem to have a form like ours, which means that, for that apparition, they either take on our form or are already in it in another dimension. There are many different places one could look for illustrations of angels appearing—both in the Old Testament and the New. An angel led Israel out of Egypt (Exodus 14:19), appeared to Daniel (Daniel 6:22), two appeared to Gideon, and so on. Angels are mentioned in many places in the New Testament, speaking and appearing to Joseph, Zechariah, Mary, Philip, Peter, Paul, and others.

It seems consistent to suppose that angels appear regularly now, too, in the normal activity of their participation with God in bringing in the kingdom. I think the writer of Hebrews accepted the presence of those outside entities calmly. Hebrews 12:1 talks about the great cloud of witnesses, or observers, who are watching us, and in Hebrews 13:2 Paul hints that we ought to be kind to strangers for we might unknowingly be entertaining angels.

Demons

There is also the picture in the Scriptures of entities who are adverse to the will of God. These entities are called demons and they, too, seem to be everywhere. Ephesians 6:12 speaks of them and says:

> . . . for we are not contending against flesh and blood, but against the principalities, against the powers, against the world rulers of this present darkness, against the spiritual hosts of wickedness in the heavenly places.

Demons are apparently fallen angels (2 Peter 2:4), are present everywhere, are seemingly working to undermine God's kingdom, and wish to inhabit people and animals. The story in Mark 5:1-13 demonstrates both of the statements in the last sentence. Demons were in a sick man in the Gerasenes' country when Jesus arrived there. He cast them out and they, after pleading and getting approval from Jesus, went into the swine. They are not seen as appearing visibly to persons in Scripture. The fact that they may not be able to appear visibly could be why they wish to inhabit someone or something else.

I have been using the word "entity" as a designation for both angels and demons. Keep in mind that entity refers to any being that has a center of consciousness within itself, that is, is its own self. There seem to be myriads of entities in existence all around us. They seem to be in their own dimension, with some having capabilities to interact with our dimension. There seem to be many dimensions of worlds. They may be like frequencies. Our world is one frequency, and there are other worlds in other frequencies. Some entities from other dimensions appear to be able to tap into ours and we can tap into theirs.

I think that the Bible dualistically breaks all entities into categories of either "angels" or "demons" just as it breaks human beings into categories of either "saved " or "lost," "redeemed" or "damned," "spiritual" or "carnal," or "he who is not with me is against me" (Matthew 12:30). Angels are entities who love God and are serving him. Demons are entities who are serving themselves and propagating evil.

If what I am suggesting is true, then the same variations, the same diversities, the same differences, and the same unlikenesses that we have in our world—from the holiest saint to the worst sinner—may also be found in the other entities that inhabit the universe. Entities "elsewhere" may be on different and numerous levels or planes and at varied stages of knowledge and development. This would explain the different opinions that come from the "outside."

In observing what has allegedly come from other entities, one can notice differences in beliefs about God, philosophy of the universe, attitudes and beliefs about creation, and opinions about death. It is as if you were hearing from a number of different people, each of whom had his or her own philosophy of life. I believe this is exactly what is happening; an outside entity's comments are just someone else's comments.

Some Christians seem to believe that if an influence is not directly of God, it is of Satan. If this is true, we have to be consistent and say it is true of persons also. There are many people whom God is using to help humankind who do not believe in him, consciously at least. Is a physician who is involved in healing, who does not believe in God, "of Satan"? I'm not sure I know anyone who could answer that affirmatively. Maybe the same is true of other entities. There may be many doing good, even though not attesting to a faith in God.

If we saw outside entity involvement only through the tunnel of demonology and witchcraft, it would be like getting a view of humankind by studying prisoners, juvenile delinquents, addicts, and sex perverts. All the variation seen in persons, in all the areas of reality that are not totally good or totally evil, may also be seen in other entities. There is increasing awareness that entities from other dimensions are speaking to us, and many are seeking to help us find a better world. Many of them may be "angels unawares," but not in the way we traditionally thought.

Guidelines for Other Entity Involvement

If other entities are actually succeeding in contacting and speaking to us, as seems to be the case, and if someday it is going to be a commonly accepted occurrence, we as Christians need to know how we feel about the matter and develop some "guidelines for involvement with entities." I believe there are some, that they make sense, and that they are clearly given to us. The guidelines are as follows:

1. *Outside entities need not be feared.* God is within us and he is greatest of all. He is the Lord of all in existence. There is plenty of Scripture that warns us to be watchful, but none that says we should be afraid, even of Satan. The Christian who is afraid of the power of evil does not understand the power of God. Some persons who preach against the occult have their audiences terrified. Where the Spirit of the Lord is, there is love and peace, not fear.

2. *Outside entities should not be revered* (treated with awe, great respect, or devotion). I think some Christians who are involved in psychic phenomena may make a mistake here. An outside word, message, or concept is not necessarily right just because it comes from the "outside." It may be just another entity's opinion or view; it should be carefully evaluated and compared with the truth we know that God has given us, just as we would do with any person's views. It

is not right just because it comes from another dimension. Related to this, Richard Neff suggests that the "reason that Biblical writers warned . . . not to visit mediums was that they could not be trusted." He cautions that what a medium conveys from the other side should not be accepted uncritically.[7]

3. *Outside entities should not be sought.* This is my own personal opinion, and I think scriptural warnings probably fit in here. In 1 Samuel 28, Saul sins by disguising himself and seeking a medium to find out the outcome of a battle. It is sin when we do not look to God. We are not even encouraged to "seek" the leading of angels.

There is evil being done by some outside entities, just as there is a lot of evil being done by some people, and to open oneself up in the seeking of an outside entity may have some very negative consequences. Certainly, following one, making decisions from one, wanting to be led by one can be very risky and dangerous. Seeking entities may open up negative levels of existence, where lower levels of entities are trying to enter into a higher level living experience. Entities seem to be limited to their own developmental level. This may be why angels can be seen, for they are on our level or above, and demons cannot. If accounts of demon possession are true, when an entity on an unhappy level gains a foothold here, it seems to hold on tenaciously and won't let go. This appears to be a situation when exorcism is necessary.

4. *If an outside entity comes to you, be open to it.* Consider an outside entity as you would another person. Hear what it says, or feel what you feel, and use, after you consider it thoughtfully and prayerfully, this information *along with* all the other information you have. If the "messages" are good and for the good of all humankind, the entity may be a messenger from God. If messages are selfish and just for personal gain, it may not be.

5. *Make God your source.* This is the most important point of all, and I have put it last for emphasis. God is ever to be our source. We are to seek him. Our faith and our searching are in him. As we seek him, *he* will send to us the entities (here and elsewhere) he assigns for our care, growth, development, and health. They are his instruments, and apparently he sends them when they are needed for our growth or care.

The sin of mediumship seems to be the sin of making other than God our source. In Deuteronomy 13:1-5 I think we can see the evil of a "psychic," or "medium," or even a "diviner" and it is that of teaching rebellion against the Lord our God. The difference between one whom we would call a prophet and one whom we would call a medium has traditionally been because the prophet was considered to be called of God, loved God, sought him, and obeyed him; and the medium was adverse to God, following his own evil ways. What if the medium loved God, felt called by God, sought him, and obeyed him, and the prophet followed his own evil intents? Then the medium would possibly be the true prophet of God and the prophet false.

We are to love God with all our hearts, souls, minds, might, and strength, and love others as ourselves. This is where it focuses. We ought to be open to every person whom God may send as a messenger of his care, however. We should not seek leading from those who do not know him and love him, but ever be mindful that he may well speak to us through such people. After we hear what others advise, we then need to seek the decision we must make in the secret of our own hearts.

In contemplating this chapter, please note your "feeling" reactions to the possibility that beings you cannot see are actively participating in your life. How individual do you think you are? Do you consider yourself to be highly predictable? Have you ever had the feeling that someone else was around when no one was visibly present? How do you feel about the guidelines for other entity involvement? Is it hard for you to imagine there may be other "beings" all around you? Does this possibility scare you or threaten you?

Chapter V

A POSSIBLE COSMOLOGY

The purpose of this chapter is to present a concept of cosmology to which I have given a lot of thought for the past couple of years. For a long time I have been looking for a possible view of the world that would allow me a conceptual framework for coordinating what I believe God is revealing through parapsychology with the gospel I embrace wholeheartedly. I understand that what we know today may need adjustment tomorrow because of new breakthroughs in research and experimentation. These "breakthroughs," in my thinking, are inspired. God is revealing more about himself and his universe all the time. There is not any way that I know of to prove many of the thoughts I will be sharing with you, and so I will not attempt to do so. The intent is to convey a possible view that to me seems to be consistent with the phenomena coming to us through parapsychology and that is also faithful to the gospel. Cosmology (in my definition) means a holistic view that allows everything to fit together in a rational way, that allows for and explains the unity, oneness, and movement of everything.

Certain aspects of the cosmology we will entertain may at first not seem to be directly related to the subject of parapsychology, but I think they are important to mention for a holistic Christian view. A

Christian cosmology, to me, should encompass most of the main teachings of the gospel to be fairly complete. A total view seems to require the consideration of the oneness of all in God, the relationship among all in God, the existence of God as a Trinity, how persons are made in the image of God, the purpose of beings God has created, God's relationship with the life he created, the fall of humankind, God's redemptive activity in Christ, and the meaning of the gospel, sin, death, and judgment.

I am not dealing with the categories just mentioned as a theologian might, with a completely thorough treatment of any of these areas. I wish only to "suggest" a possible conceptual framework for understanding the universe that is open to discoveries occurring in the field of parapsychology and also faithful to the gospel.

Each person is at a different place in his or her growth and development. Some Christians may be satisfied with traditional Christian thought frameworks for generations to come. Others may not. I believe there are many different ways to understand God's activity and workings, and I have found for myself a lot of enjoyment in exploring different personal views wherein my faith can be increased with every new discovery and advancement.

The thoughts contained in this part of the book are simply my exploratory "thinking out loud." The thinking is different from most of my theological background, but yet to me carries the gospel message as always. I am a Christian, fully committed to God through Christ, and am increasingly excited about what God has been and is doing in the world. God and his universe are so far beyond us that it is difficult to think that we are even partially understanding them; yet God seems to have always revealed himself and his plans for us in ways that, at least for a time, seem very clear. I see each part of this chapter as a question to you and to me, "Could it be this way?"

All Things One

I find myself looking for a view that shows the oneness of all that exists—person with person, person with environment, and person with God. I believe everything is interconnected and that there is a continual and unique "exchange" of life going on incessantly. There are different dimensions, and these dimensions make up a whole. For me, present research has unquestionably proved these things, but how does that fit into Christian theology?

Edgar Mitchell feels that we have viewed the universe as "a whole thing which we have arbitrarily divided into compartments by disciplines." However, he feels that "a holistic multidisciplinary approach to research is needed."[1] I believe Christians can find that approach if they can open their thinking to new possibilities. We do not need concepts that change the Christian faith but ones that explain it in different ways, that even understand it in different ways.

The thoughts I present in this chapter cannot be proven any more than any "faith" construct, but I anticipate that these ideas might help you to see how one can be committed to Christ and the gospel and still be creatively active in different ways of understanding that belief.

A general theme appearing and reappearing in many parapsychological articles is that of "oneness." Professor of Astrophysical Sciences at Princeton University, Dr. Jeremiah P. Ostriker indicates that many times in physics two things are considered different, each a "conserved quantity." Later it is discovered that they are really "different manifestations of the same thing" and that their sum is the "conserved quantity." One thing therefore changes into another.[2]

In an interview, Robert H. Dicke, Cyrus Fogg Brackett Professor of Physics, was asked if particles are really particles or if they are bits of energy. His answer was that actually these two terms, "particles" and "bits of energy," describe the same thing. He feels that the only way a thing can be described is by the way it behaves. He also feels that scientists have begun to change their theories about the nature of physical particles. Not too long ago people thought the proton, neutron, and electron were definite particles created at the beginning of creation. Though one could change into another, they each had a definite existence. He went on to mention that today a more common view is that the particle is a continuingly changing form that has quite a complex structure. For example, neutrons are sometimes neutrons and at other times protons, electrons, and neutrons. He sees this exchange as a very complex idea which involves particles which form and reform and dissolve into each other. He feels that one day scientists will formulate the theory that all elementary particles are actually different forms of the same thing and that these particles are able to take different forms.[3]

Olga Worrall, a very sophisticated faith healer who speaks frequently for the Academy of Parapsychology and Medicine, made a statement that impressed me:

There is a "something" out of which comes everything. . . . This certain "something" is neither energy nor matter but is the source of both. It has neither magnitude nor dimension. It is both timeless and spaceless.[4]

To her, this is God. Others would not say it is God, but would recognize the existence of this primary "something."

John Lilly, who breaks down psychic experiences into different levels, states that out of his experiences he has become aware that all Essences are joined to each other on the higher levels and communicate with each other with or without the knowledge of one's self. It is only as persons move deeper into their own Essences that they discover this strong connection between their own Essences and all other Essences.[5]

In his book *The One Quest,* Claudio Naranjo includes some of Alan Watts's thoughts. Watts feels that every person is an expression of, a unique action of, the whole universe. He does not think most individuals ever experience that. Even if we can develop the concept in theory, we still seem to be aware of ourselves "as isolated 'egos' inside bags of skin." He sees the result of our seeing ourselves as isolated persons as being the cause of much of the hostility in the world. We are always wanting to conquer nature rather than cooperate with it.[6]

In considering the psyche, Carl Jung believes that in one sense psyches are not individual but come from the total of humanity. He sees us in some way as being part of one psyche.[7]

Quincy Howe, Jr., Associate Professor of Classics at Scripps College, says that he believes that the person who makes the proper effort will most likely succeed in recognizing that separation from God is an illusion and the impression of fragmentation and estrangement is a deception. He sees all as one, "as heat and light are both one with the sun."[8]

Claudio Naranjo feels that the difference between the religious approach to the self and the psychological is that the religious approach goes beyond seeing the person as just an individual entity. He thinks that if persons really see into themselves, they will find themselves to be just drops in an infinite ocean of existence. Humankind is a "microcosm replicating the whole macrocosm" and a person's soul is one with the soul of everything, under the illusion of individual existence.[9]

Stanley Krippner has developed some concepts that show how certain of these recognitions of the oneness of all things have practical psychological and sociological implications. He relates that it took many hundreds of thousands of years for human beings to learn to write their language. He wonders how much longer it will take for them to learn to use their own psi. He thinks the time will be much shorter between the discovery of the psi and an application of the discovery in the coming years. He sees the new awarenesses as lessening the alienation we have from each other, allowing for more psychic unity and thus for more closeness than ever before conceived. He thinks that due to our psychic potential we are more closely connected than our physical boundaries would indicate. He entertains the possibility that all of life is interrelated in ways which we do not yet comprehend. He feels as we develop more insight into this linkage through parapsychological research we will better understand how much we are a part of each other and how much we need each other. This may greatly decrease the cruelty and exploitation that exist among humans.[10]

The physicist, the philosopher, the religionist, as well as the parapsychologist are seemingly finding more and more evidence of the oneness and unity of all in existence, and are looking for the development of a view that will "take it all into account."

God, the Primary Substance

To the Christian the primary something, the basic person, element, factor, entity, reality of life, or substance, is God. Most Christians would heartily agree that God is that from which all comes; but what that means may lead to many differences. Here are just a few verses from the Bible that lead us to believe that God is the source of all: Acts 17:28, "In him we live and move and have our being"; Job 12:10, "In his hands is the life of every living thing and the breath of all mankind"; Ephesians 4:6, "One God and Father of us all, who is above all and through all and in all"; 1 Corinthians 8:6, "Yet for us there is one God, the Father, from whom are all things and for whom we exist, and one Lord, Jesus Christ, through whom are all things and through whom we exist"; Colossians 1:16-17, "For in him all things were created, in heaven and on earth, visible and invisible, whether thrones or dominions or principalities or authorities—all things were created through him and for him. He is before all things, and in him all things hold together."

God is the essence of all in existence. All things come from God. He is the basic substance from which all life exists. It exists because of him and from him. He is in life and it cannot exist without him, and thus all that exists must in some sense be an extension of him. Nothing can exist on its own except God, and in God's existence, or from God's existence, emanates all life. All that exists is not God, but it cannot be separated from him for it cannot exist without him.

To say there is life that God does not animate is to say there is life that animates itself, and thus it does not need God. I believe that God is that which animates all life and therefore he is the life of all life. It exists because he exists. Nothing can exist without him.

We need God's wisdom, or the ability to accept a mystery that is seemingly a paradox, to understand how all can be a part of God and not be God. Pantheism erroneously equates the physical universe with God, limiting God to the universe. All that exists is not God, but God has within himself, or as a part of himself, all that is. All that exists is in a sense an extension of God. All that is, is of him, from him, and in him, but he is more than all that.

What exists in him appears to be in many different forms within the basic categories of matter (or form), spirit, and thought. All may be a different "arrangement" of the primary substance which is God. For example, the creation of our physical-material world was possibly a changing in the state of this primary substance. It has appeared as if something were created out of nothing, but really it might have been a transformation of the state of that substance.

God is the macrocosm; everything else is a microcosm. If we include everything, there are myriads of microcosms that are a part of God, who is the whole of all the parts, and more. He is not all the parts; the parts are a part of him. There seem to be countless variations of the primary substance of God, countless dimensions, levels, platitudes, frequencies; call them what you may. On each level there seems to be form, spirit, and thought. The reality we know in the life experience we have here may be like no more than one narrow frequency on a radio band. There may be thousands of others.

Robert Ornstein uses the chart of the electromagnetic spectrum to point out that the visual spectrum is but one tiny slit in the whole energy band. This electromagnetic spectrum includes wavelengths which range from less than one billionth of a meter to wavelengths which measure more than a thousand meters. However, we can see only those wavelengths which are between 400 and 700 billionths of a meter. He also points out other factors in addition to electromagnetic energy, such as mechanical vibrations in the air, gaseous matter, etc., that the eye is totally ignorant of. He makes the observation that we could not possibly experience the world as it really exists—that we would be overwhelmed. Our physical bodies are able to relate to only a few sensory dimensions.[11]

If this is true of just the physiological world, how much more would it be applicable as showing the possibilities of the total universe with all its possibility and breadth?

The three categories of reality—form, spirit, and thought—could correspond with possible conceptions we might have of God as a Trinity. A way of looking at God might be to see him as having form, spirit, and thought. God's form may be all that exists as form (all physical-material reality). His spiritual reality may be all that exists that is spirit. His mental reality may be all that exists that is mind or thought. In each of these areas, though, there is a transcendence of God beyond the statements just made, so that God cannot be said to "be" all form, all spirit, all thought. All that exists is in God, but he is more than the totality.

Jesus Christ could be seen to be the "specific" form of God. Colossians 1:15 states, "He is the image of the invisible God." Generally speaking, however, we might see the "whole" form of God as we conceive our own physical bodies. All form (nature) may be God's body like our bodies are ours. This aspect of God is similar to that portion of our bodies which exists and works without our conscious involvement—the autonomic part. This is what I call the consistency of God's "body."

Jesus Christ, as the specific form of God, seems to be the instrument of the "arranging" of all other form in God. The Scriptures seem definitely to attribute to him the creation of things in heaven and on earth (Colossians 1:15-19). There are places in the Old Testament, such as Exodus 33:34, that seem to show Christ's existence in a form, so one may think he indeed might always have had form—the specific form of God who created all other form (realities, such as our physical-material world). All other realms appear also to have this form aspect, too. It is observed in the concept of heaven in particular.

God's "body" may then be all that exists that is in a form. It is not he, but it is in him and is a part of him. Jesus Christ is the body of God that is "his own," distinct from the other.

God's "spirit" may be all that exists as spirit. This might be called the life energy (for want of a better term) of God. All that exists lives by the active reality of God's spirit bringing life. This is God's presence everywhere as the source and sustenance of life itself. It is the totality of all that exists that is not form or thought. All spirit is in God and is of God. His spirit seems to connect all spirit and is the spirit of all life. All spirit, though, is not God, for God has, beyond "all spirit," a spirit life which is his own. That spirit which is his own, apart from the spirit connecting and sustaining all life, is possibly designated in the Scriptures as the "Holy Spirit."

God as the "heavenly Father" could be seen as the thought reality of God. Even the concept of heavenly Father is a thought concept. One uses the process of thinking to imagine what a Father is like. The Scriptures clearly state that no one has seen God at any time. Some commentators believe the reference is to God the Father. No one has seen God the Father, but Jesus, who was seen, has made him known (see John 1:18).

Maybe the heavenly Father is the thought reality of God. (In the last chapter I will discuss the possibility that thoughts are "real things " and maybe the original or beginning form from which all emanates.) All thought may be in God's thought, but he has thought beyond that, which is uniquely "his own." The "his own" would be his own specific consciousness. God's thought, then, may be all that exists as thought or mind. It is not he, but it is in him and is a part of him. God has a consciousness that is his own, though, and it is seen as the activity of the heavenly Father.

One can never live apart from the thought, spirit, or form of God because one lives *because* of the thought, spirit, and form of God. One can experience, however, a personal encounter with the thought, spirit, and form of God, just as one can live without an awareness that all one is, is because God is. A personal encounter with God would be a personal relationship with that part of God that is "other" than us. It would be our conscious contact with his consciousness, our spirit knowing his Holy Spirit, and our form knowing the form of Jesus Christ. You might say then that to be in conscious union with God is to be experiencing the personal self of God in a specific way.

Let me reiterate: all that exists, then, emanates from God. It exists because of him and it exists in him. It is in a sense a part of him and could not "be" at all without him. All is a partial existence of his complete existence. All is in a way God's body, God's spirit, and God's mind. But God is more than that; he is also himself. He transcends all the "parts" as a marvelous being who exists with his own Selfhood.

The oneness between people, people and animals, animals and plants, plants and people, etc., exists because all are one in God and all are the same basic substance, though in a different form or "arrangement." The oneness of all might be analogous to the oneness of the muscles, tendons, nerves, blood, cells, eyes, etc., of the human body. The unlikeness of the examples is intentional, for even though plants, animals, and human beings don't seem naturally to have any oneness other than being in the same world, they are one in the reality of the whole.

All the various forms, spirits, and minds are possibly all interconnected and joined in him. You cannot really separate anything in existence from anything else in existence, and each aspect or part of existence is in interaction with the other parts, to give to each other life in God. That which exists, in a process of unique interchange, provides everything else its existence. We are receiving from and giving to everything else all the time. As plants give us oxygen to breathe and we give plants carbon dioxide to "breathe," so is there an apparent continual exchange of all life with all other life, and thus in God, all are one.

This concept finds importance within the awareness of parapsychological researchers: that nothing seems to exist in isolation. Everything is possibly one. As in our own individuality, our bodies, spirits, and minds are one, and ineluctably intertwined, so are all forms, all spirits, all minds; and so are all minds connected with all spirits and all spirits with all forms. This interchange of life may occur between all dimensions and levels of existence, too. Most of the dynamics of this interchange do not seem to be consciously experienced, but we are learning more and more how to be more conscious of these marvelous interactions, exchanges, and interconnections in God. It is not difficult to understand people relating to plants and plants to people; minds relating to other minds without conventional communication, even contact with intelligence from other dimensions, etc., when you see everything being one in God. Even if one is not consciously aware of it, it would still be occurring.

As Christians, we don't want to make the same error the Israelites made in thinking we are "it." We are not "it." The whole of all that God created is "it," and we are able consciously to participate in helping others see and know the One who is giving them life. It is because of the presence of God's Spirit that all life "lives and moves and has its being." The "specific" life of God is given to those who "call upon him in holiness," but his life in general is everywhere and is the life of everything. As Peter had to acknowledge that the Holy Spirit was also given to the Gentiles (Acts 10:34-35), so many of us may need to realize that God's life is the very substance of everyone's living whether one acknowledges it or not. This is why many people who do not seem to know God personally can and do feel his presence and can enjoy certain experiences with God through nature (see Romans 1:20).

Independent Beings

God created everything from himself and evidently created certain aspects of it with a character of independence wherein a center of consciousness, or independence or self-awareness, could exist. Parapsychologists call this an "entity." The entity has a unique "I am me" element wherein it is aware of the independence of itself. Although life cannot exist without God, it can exist, therefore, in entities without their having a conscious awareness of him.

The lifetime of God is the lifetime of all life. That is, if all life emanates from God, it was always "in" him. There have apparently been times of certain transformations that have brought "new" awarenesses into existence, but they have possibly only started existing as a changed state, not a beginning. As far as we know, nothing ends. A present state ends, but a transformation is actually occurring wherein that which we think has ended has merely moved to a different state. For example, water becomes gas as it is heated, and the gas is dissipated into the air but is never ultimately lost. All beings have always existed in God, as has everything.

Beings seem to exist in countless numbers, in countless forms, in countless places. Apparently, all persons are in the process of "becoming," and the becoming is within the framework of infinite possibilities within God. All of life, in fact, seems to be in a constant transition, in a continual movement. The person is an experiencing subject and is constituted by its experiences. Its experiences result from its own selection of the number of possibilities at any given moment and by the consequences or building of its selections up to that moment. Each entity is "becoming" as it learns from and responds to its own experience. In *Science and the Modern World,* Alfred North Whitehead develops some of these concepts most expertly. Some of them are combined with mine on the following pages.

John Cobb, in *A Christian Natural Theology*, states:

> In Whitehead's view, therefore, the soul [person] is not at all like a substance undergoing accidental adventures in time. It is constituted by its adventures. It can attain richness and depth only through the variety and quality of the entities it encounters and its own willingness and ability to be open to what they can contribute.[12]

God seems to give impetus to the entity to "self-create," to "want to experience." The entity is in a process of self-information, with "subjective aim," or a feeling of what the process may achieve. In other words, God puts within the being an interest in what its life comes to. This can surely be seen in our searching for meaning and happiness. A person who is not interested in his/her own life is generally considered a person deficient of the necessary "stuff" needed for a meaningful living. I know from counseling that suicide can sometimes be explained by this loss of interest in what one's life experiences. It is very difficult to counsel with someone who has no interest in what happens to him or her. This is an unnatural state and is a negative life position.

God's influence is related to our prehension of him. That is, God is supremely attractive and beautiful and by this persuasive magnitude is leading persons to his higher thoughts, feelings, and values. The direct influence of God may possibly be analogous to the power of thought over thought and feeling over feeling. It is the power of inspiration and suggestion.

Entities continue to "advance themselves" under God's encouragement and stimulation. God is leading us to expand our awareness of ourselves and our potential. Today in our contemporary human situation, God seems to be opening up the appetites of many for awareness experiences with a wider range of reality than the physical-material world holds, and this is partly seen in the interest in parapsychology. On every level of existence, even those other than ours, there is probably the reaching out for more knowledge, experience, awareness, and reality; for God probably has given all of life an inner desire, like his own, to grow, to expand, to create, to be more.

The beings, themselves, may determine their rate of awareness and development, and possibly do it by their responses to the stimulation of God. God is leading and guiding entities to find and accept his values. Ultimately, the finding of these values is the zenith enjoyment of being a person or an entity. As persons respond to the present, they determine the "rate" of their growth toward the full experiencing of that which God experiences within himself.

Beings can limit themselves by not being interested in using each opportunity to its fullest, or they can be limited by the selection of possibilities at any given moment. God seems to control or limit an entity's selection of possibilities when necessary to assure the movement of the universe in its proper direction. Entities may also be limited by the society in which they exist. That is, the more persons conform to their environment, the more their rate of development will coincide with that environment. They will develop only as fast as the society in which they exist develops. The more persons respond and make choices and decisions through their own subjective element, the less restriction and more possibilities there will be. Beings can find growth, freedom, and creativity to almost any degree they wish to open themselves up to.

God's plan for entities seems to be for persons to discover their individuality, uniqueness, self-worth, and personal value, and at the same time to discover their unity or oneness with all other life. This is to discover how marvelously persons are "themselves" and at the same time discover how much they are a part of everything else, too. The important thing is *being*—being a self and being a part of the whole. "Being" involves full awareness of yourself as a distinct "I am" and a full awareness of yourself as a "part of the whole" universe. It seems a paradox, but it is not. One can become more and more individual and more and more universal at the same time.

I want to say a little more about God's leading entities to the realization of his dreams and values. In bringing this to fruition, God seems to use evolution *and* specific action. As we observe history, we see natural events that seem to evolve or emanate according to the natural laws of God's body (nature), and events that seem to originate from the conscious intention or action of God. There should be no diversity between a concept of evolution and the direct activity of a personal God, for both can be true. God seemed to form some things that "carry themselves" by the natural sequencing of evolving consequences or effects, and some things that result from his direct activity. The kingdom of heaven, then, may be coming by both natural evolution and the specific action of God. You might say that within the continuance of the movement of life are specific times when God activates transformations that bring about specific events that expedite the coming of his kingdom. The Bible shows us precise events at seemingly definite points or times or places that fit into the unfolding of the coming of the kingdom of God. Life basically seems to be a consistent "becoming" with no interest in hurrying for some of the beings who become impatient.

God's incarnation in Jesus as a human, actually experiencing the same physical-material world we do, was his ultimate stimulative act. His life shows us how to live, how to love, how to be uniquely ourselves, but at the same time be one with God and the world. His death shows us the results or consequences of evil, the extent of God's love, the cost of forgiveness, and the way to face death. His resurrection shows us that death is merely a transition and that life continues after death in another form.

The Continuance of Life

All life seems to continue in constant movement. Things change form but continue in existence. This leads us to a discussion about the continuance of life, not only from the concept of after physical birth, but also in consideration of pre-birth possibility. We are talking about the question of whether a person might have existed prior to this physical-material experience. It interests me that Christians can believe so readily in the eternity of life after birth in a physical body, but not think of eternity and existence prior to this.

There are generally three possible positions to take in reference to persons who continue eternally coming into a physical experience. Either the persons existed previously and came into physical bodies, or the persons develop for the first time with the development of a physiology in the womb, or they are directly created by God at some point and "put" into physical bodies sometime before or at birth.

The reason the continuance of life concept is going to be a major section of this part of the book is that there are many in the field of parapsychology beginning to give it very serious consideration. An example is Robert A. Bradley, M.D., who practices obstetrics and gynecology in Denver and who says that today he is personally convinced that there was a life prior to this one and that this can be used as a therapeutic tool in teaching people to adjust to their present-day problems. Another example was given in the March 4, 1974, *Time* magazine. It states that psychiatrist Ian Stevenson, of the University of Virginia Medical School, is studying the plausibilities of reincarnation. An English psychiatrist, Dr. Kelsey, who practices in New York, uses hypnotic regression in therapy. Dr. Douglas Dean also affirms his belief in pre-birth possibility.[13] The fact that some kind of a concept of "reincarnation" is believed by so many (millions of people have embraced it over the centuries, particularly in the East), and so many psychics believe it and speak of knowing it by awareness of people's "other lives" and from contact with those on the "other side," has called attention to its possibility.

Christians have traditionally denied the possibility of reincarnation. The Bible, however, says very little about it directly, either pro or con. Certain biblical passages, though, indicate that the return of a person, especially a prophet, was an accepted belief. In Matthew 16:13-16, it shows that people thought Jesus was a prophet returned. Those were apparently serious suggestions. In Matthew 17:10-13, Jesus indicated fairly clearly that John the Baptist was Elijah come back. In Luke 9:7-9, Herod was willing to accept the possibility that one from the past had come back. In John 9:2, the disciples asked about a blind man: "Rabbi, who sinned, this man or his parents, that he was born blind?" Jesus answered, "Neither." Apparently they believed the man could have sinned before his birth. A good book on this subject is *The Belief in a Life After Death* by Curt John Ducasse. A part of the book gives a fairly thorough critical examination of reincarnation. Ducasse mentions the fact that Origen, one of the most influential early Church Fathers in the development of Christian theology, held "that the human soul preexisted and in some sense lived prior to its entrance into the body, but also after death it eventually reentered a new body, and this repeatedly until . . . it was fit to enter heaven."[14]

Another book on the subject of reincarnation is the current (1974) book of Quincy Howe, Jr., called *Reincarnation for the Christian.* In his book the author readily accepts the responsibility of firmly stating his belief in this truth or teaching. Howe seeks as explicitly as possible to indicate the theological and metaphysical assumptions upon which the doctrine of reincarnation is based. He points out, as Ducasse did, that Christians have not given serious thought to the possibility of reincarnation since the Council of 553 when Origen, who espoused the doctrine, was banned.[15]

The author asks us to answer a question he had to answer for himself, which is this: "How far can one deviate from the accepted norms of Christian belief without threatening the very source and substance of his religious life?" The answer he apparently found for himself was that as one would reduce the Christian life to its bare essentials, he or she would discover that the first concern of the Christian is not doctrine, for a person can live a life in Christ and be subject to the will of God within a very wide range of beliefs.[16]

Quincy Howe makes a few other comments that might be appropriate to mention. He feels that many Christians find doctrine to play an ambiguous and even obstructive role in their religious life. He thinks too often the religious life begins with statements of creed and doctrine rather than the experience with God from which doctrine should be a reflection. He sees some Christians who have experiences and intuitions that seem to support that which is not traditional or orthodox as being very frustrated, for the doctrine of the church tells them they are wrong, while their own inner voices assure them of the contrary.[17] The measure of a person's faith may not be one's orthodoxy as much as the capacity of that faith to arouse others to a life in Christ. It may be that we fight so hard to keep from believing some possible variations of our faith, which might make it even more meaningful, that we bypass truths God would have us embrace that are necessary for our continued growth and development.

I am not attempting to prove this concept, for I don't think anyone can prove or disprove it. Personally, I find myself more and more responding to the thought that life is a "continuing experience." I don't especially like the word "reincarnation" because it speaks of growth and development occurring only in the earth experience. This word in itself is a block to many people. The continuance of life concept sees a person as a totality of all his or her experiences, whether in or out of a physical-material construct as we have here. I find deep meaning in consideration of the continuance of life concept as to its progress, or the intent of its process. The gospel can be seen very meaningfully within it, and I hope to be able to convey some of this possible meaning so that a believer will not feel he or she has to choose *either* a Christian position *or* a continuance of life position.

The Kingdom of God

In my own thinking, we have to begin with a conception of what the kingdom of heaven will be like. It is, to me, an existence, or a state of existence, wherein everyone who is a part of it loves God with the whole heart, soul, mind, might, and strength, and loves everyone else and seeks their benefit and well-being equally with his or her own. This state or level of existence exists because everyone there has come to realize that this is the best way for life to be. In other words, by experience, each knows that God's way, his will, his life-style (if you wish) is the best.

Through an experience of knowing good and evil (Genesis 3:22), those in the kingdom of heaven may have come to realize that good is supremely superior to evil and that is what they want. Of their own volition, now they consistently want good. They remain faithful to God's ways now because they, through much experience, know God's ways are best. They have come to love God deeply and to enjoy the closeness they feel to him and the oneness they are experiencing with his world. They remain continually conscious of the enduring patience God showed to them during their existence, the extent to which he went to draw them unto himself, even to the extent of his activity in and through Christ.

As beings respond to God, therefore, they are involved in their own self-formation and thus also in the formation of God's kingdom. The coming of the kingdom is in direct relation to the understanding of entities and their response to God. This is undoubtedly why its coming is effected by the spreading of the "Good News." Jesus said the gospel must first be spread to the ends of the earth. I am not sure this refers to geography as much as to persons hearing, responding, and being changed by the gospel.

The biblical picture of humankind's environment before the Fall is one of oneness. Adam and Eve were one with God and their surroundings. Peace, harmony, unity, and ease are just a few words that might depict the atmosphere of their situation prior to their encounter with the "other possibility," evil. The story of the Fall of humankind is the story of persons moving away from harmony with their whole environment (meaning God, themselves, others, the world, the animals, everything). Their independence resulted in their violation of the oneness of the universe, and they joined God in knowing what happens when one does violate God's life. This violation set off a series of reactions that would continue for centuries, until by their own volition persons would again choose this oneness. God takes the initiative, but we must respond.

Congruence, wholeness, and oneness gave way to incongruence, dissipation, and dissension. Instead of warmth and closeness came coldness and loneliness. The most serious consequences relate to feelings of isolation, being cut off from God. Many individuals would say, rather, that they are cut off from meaning, purpose, and happiness. Feeling cut off from God is possibly an illusion—an illusion that leads to a fact created by the illusion itself. We cut ourselves off from God. We create our own disharmony and disunity. Jesus' experience with sin had this same effect. When on the cross he felt cut off and cried out, "My God, my God, why have you forsaken me?", God had not forsaken him, as we know. But Jesus surely experienced that most intense consequence of sin, feeling completely cut off from his Father.

Jesus demonstrated a life fully consistent with God's life. He moved with his heavenly Father every moment. There were no obstructions, no incongruencies, no inconsistencies. He showed us the potential of a life flowing in perfect harmony with God, and therefore all that is possible in God is seen. Adam violated the laws of God and showed us the consequences, and we experience the consequences. Jesus was one with God and showed and continues to show us the consequences of that oneness, and we can experience that. As Adam's disobedience grew, so Jesus' obedience is growing. Jesus' life is growing in the coming of the kingdom of God. The signs of the coming of his kingdom are men and women loving God and each other, and out of that love emanates life consistent with God's laws, or universal principles of oneness.

In summary, then, before the Fall of humankind we see the results of oneness, harmony, and unity. After the Fall we see the consequences of the violation of God. In Jesus we see again what wholeness means; it whets our appetites and we want it.

The Fall of Humankind and the Gospel

The consequences of the Fall of humankind are not without meaning. In experiencing them, we (and other entities in their own way, I suppose) see and feel the results of the violation. This is because of a law that God has established: you reap what you sow. This is what I call the "law of consequences." Galatians 6:7 shows us this law: "Do not be deceived, God is not mocked, for whatever a man sows, that he will also reap." This law of God cannot be overlooked or circumvented. This law is not punishment. It is the experiencing yourself what you have been doing to violate life, so that you can:

1. See the wrong of it—that it doesn't work;
2. Feel its effects on persons and life;
3. Feel sorry for violation of God's law and life;
4. Change.

We apparently experience the consequences of our violations of life until we have realized the wrongness of our violations and have moved to correct them in our attitudes and living. The Christian message is that in the whole life and death of Christ we have the ultimate objective exposure of the consequences of evil. By an encounter with him it is possible for us to realize the four points above (the purpose of experiencing the violation done) and thus bypass the consequences.

The experience of persons encountering themselves and God is clearly seen in the Christian gospel. Whether these steps occur in one lifetime or in many lifetimes does not seem to change its message or efficacy. We know, however, that in many it has not occurred in this lifetime. It has not occurred in many who call themselves believers either. Some believers do not seem ready for heaven if heaven is as we previously described the kingdom of heaven. Some believers are still hating, remaining selfish and self-centered, and are violating God's will. Jesus said that if we do not forgive, we will not be forgiven (Matthew 6:14-15). He also said that if we are not compassionate and considerate of others, even strangers, we are not ready for the kingdom of heaven (Matthew 25:35-46). I think that there may be much that many of us will yet have to learn before we are ready for residence in the kingdom of heaven. By this, I do not mean to suggest we "work" our way into heaven, but rather that we have to understand the gospel and be committed to it to become a part of it. The living of many of us may indicate we do not yet really understand what we need to understand to be there.

I believe that all spiritual searching is initiated by God. He is drawing his creation unto himself. Entities exist in a continuing fashion, and in their existence God is encountered in many different ways. Many of these ways are general, as in nature. If they respond to this aspect of God's initiative, he begins to encounter them in more specific ways, such as through other persons, in overt modes of communication (such as preaching and reading). Then when they begin to conceptualize him as a being that is himself, God moves their hearts to know him as a person.

Jesus Christ seems to be the focal point for consciously knowing God as a person. Jesus is a "man of our world," and we encounter God consciously in him. He epitomizes God's message to all generations, and it is in him one meets God. Knowing God is an encounter with the consciousness of God wherein one being meets another, and wherein entities, conscious of their own being, meet the entity that gave them being. Consciousness meets consciousness, and an aware personal experience begins.

To know about God, therefore, and to feel and experience him, or to know he is with you and around you, is not all there is; you can meet him personally and he will be not only your God but also your friend and continual companion. The first sequencing of events in the continuing life of an entity is for the purpose of encountering God as a person in the way I have described above. The second sequencing of events seems, then, to be for the purpose of adjusting oneself to the new conscious life in God. For me, the cross symbolizes this encounter, and the language of the cross, as spoken by Christ in the Garden of Gethsemane where he struggled, symbolizes what the encounter means: "Not my will but Thy will be done." The encounter is an encounter with your own self, your own intentions, your own will, as it relates to God's own self, his intentions, and his will. It is the question of whether one will remain in incongruence to the flow of God's life, and thus the life of the universe, or become a conscious part of God's life and thus one with the universe.

At this point I will include a diagram that will probably help you see a better picture of what I am discussing with you. (See the following page.)

This diagram could have included so many different things or could have been done in so many different ways. I believe that some people, maybe many, can have an encounter (a conscious one) with God through Christ in a sequence (or progression) of awarenesses, as we have just mentioned, that leads them to a life-changing experience with God, without their even being consciously aware of who Jesus Christ is, in terms of a formulated doctrine or faith. Christ is the initiator of all genuine spiritual experience. Whether one is consciously aware of this or not may not be as critical as many Christians believe. The issue is: "What has happened to the entity that has encountered God?" If there is deep and genuine love for God and other persons (even though God may be conceptualized a bit differently), it would seem to be of God's Spirit with Jesus Christ as the initiator of it. Sometimes we may put too much emphasis on the "head" part (formulated doctrine), often to the exclusion of the life God wants us to live. From the continuance of life concept, genuine persons seeking God, will, in this life or another time, meet, know, and accept the One (Christ) leading them in their spiritual journey.

Not My Will but Thy Will Be Done

1. Learning that selfishness, evil, etc., do not work (they rob or detract from life)

2. Experiencing the effects of evil (hurt, loneliness, emptiness, pain, etc.)

3. Feeling sorry for your violation of life (beginning to see another way)

4. Wanting to be changed (ready for an encounter with God)

1. Learning God's will (finding out what he wants)

2. Learning to go with God (experiencing him talking to and leading you)

3. Learning to love him and others

4. Being active in the coming of his kingdom

The Encounter with Yourself and God

(Includes in one form or another)

1. Awareness of God as a person you can know
2. Realization of your violation of his life
3. Admittance of violations and desire to change
4. Conscious commitment to his ways, his will
5. The experience of consciously meeting God
6. The experience of wishing now to know him better

Repentance is realizing the destructive and obstructive elements of our lives and wishing to change them or have them changed. It is realization to the extent of motivating us to want to repair what we can (Zacchaeus, for example, was willing to pay back everyone he had cheated as a tax collector). Forgiveness is God's response to repentance; it is his healing of the "damage" done to the entity by negative living. When we oppose God's order of the universe (sin), we are judged immediately. We are judged by ourselves, and the effects occur in ourselves. This is what we are calling the law of consequences. What we do (acts, thoughts, attitudes, and behavior) immediately affects us.

Quincy Howe states this in his concepts about *karma*. He sees *karma* as an active working or action. It is an effect that results from some prior activity. He sees *karma* as a continuing series of causes and effects which affects existence at all levels. He relates Newton's Third Law of Motion "for every action there is an equal and opposite reaction" as being a factor for not just the mechanical and physical universe, but true also for the realms of the emotions, the mind, and the spirit. He feels that all thoughts and deeds affect the equilibrium of the universe and require a response.[18]

Forgiveness is a corrective happening wherein repair or healing occurs. It may sometimes be so complete, if allowed to be realized to full fruition, that the consequences of the violation of life no longer show ("though your sins be as scarlet, they shall be as white as snow").

Conversion, or the new life, occurs when a person stops living in opposition to, or incongruence with, God's life and begins to become one with him (John 17). The initial occurrence often seems to bring great relief and peace, for one joins the flow of the universe instead of opposing it (like swimming with the current rather than against it). In the flow of God's life one finds God's love, care, and guidance; for *everything* existing has God's purpose. Nothing is without meaning except that which has not yet discovered its meaning. This is a great discernment, for there is no large or small, big or little, to God. He is in the smallest atom and in the grandeur of the whole universe. Being in the whole necessitates being in the parts. God is as interested in every detail of our lives as he is in the whole of our lives. Each detail is a part, and all the parts make up the total way we are; thus, to be interested at all is to be interested in all.

There often seem to be what some people call "superficial conversions" that occur from a present state of hurt or frustration.

These encounters with God seem to be only temporary, and when the hurt or frustration is past, so is interest in flowing with God. However, these superficial conversions may not be superficial at all; they may be just a part of a person's experiences with God that will eventually lead to a permanent "new life." We become bothered by this only when we think within a "time pressure" framework. At least for certain periods of time these persons realized the value of seeking and experiencing God. One day they may recognize the value of remaining permanently in him. When one has experienced many single encounters with God that are very fulfilling and personally salutary, one will begin to have a permanent appetite for this closeness. This may be seen as the continued way God leads persons unto himself.

I want to say a little more about the continuance of life concept. This one physical life may be just a small part of our whole "life." What makes it difficult to sort out, as to whether there is one physical-material life here or several physical-material life experiences here that comprise the total of our physical-material life experiences, is that within a single life the whole drama of all life is seen. The gospel could be a message to a being with one physical-material life experience or to a being with several such life experiences and not need to be changed one bit. It speaks to one about life, "period." Life is where you are now, at the point you are now, the responses you have now. Whether a person lives one physical life or several, the message is the same.

I think it is reasonable to entertain the possibility that beings encounter many different forms, dimensions, places, and experiences other than, as well as, this one existence, and that all of these comprise the "life" of the person. Quincy Howe expresses it by indicating what we are now is the "composite of layer upon layer of experience" some of which disappears from conscious memory, but which always leaves the traces.[19] I am aware that this is not a common Christian attitude or position. It took me quite a while to be able to espouse its possibility with my friends and fellow Christians. This concept now, though, could fit into my Christian faith and provide me with an understanding of certain things I had difficulty understanding before. For example: Those chosen for specific tasks or places of importance (Romans 9, related to Jacob and Esau; John 17, related to the choice of the disciples) may have been chosen as a result of their overall previous pattern of response to God. In

Matthew 16:28 Jesus says that some who were standing there with him would not taste death before they saw the Son of man coming in his kingdom. Jesus obviously was not referring to a particular physical-material death of the body.

Physical Death, Sin, and Judgment

The termination of a physical body is a transition, not a death. Hebrews 9:27 says: "And just as it is appointed unto men to die once, and after that comes the judgment." The words "to die once" may not refer to a very temporary physiology. In the Old Testament in particular there seems to be a real indifference in respect for life; that is, masses were killed by the apparent direction of God. If the death of the physical body is merely a transition wherein the entity continues to grow, develop, and experience, then it is not as much of a tragedy. The tragedy is the death of the "person" whenever and if ever that occurs.

If, after the end of a physical existence, an entity continues to evaluate that experience and can learn from it, a life or several lives can be a tremendous classroom for learning. William Tiller uses this analogy of the classroom, for he believes we function in a non-time, non-space aspect, and that there is the development of a coherence in ourselves by the experiences we have. Many of these experiences, he believes, take place in a space-time classroom where we presently find ourselves.

Fear of death may occur when persons have not achieved or realized what has been intended for them to achieve and realize, and thus they are not "ready" to die. I know many Christians who are very much afraid to die. I also know others, though, who appear to have completed their "assignment" for this stage of their development, for they simply slip out smoothly and peacefully. If one violates his or her life, he or she can die before he or she has achieved his or her purpose, and that is a fearful thing. Persons who respond to the leading of God in their lives will find no fear at the termination of their physical-material bodies.

Entities who are responsive to God's stimulation in their becoming will continue to grow, to develop, and to love God and one another. Beings who are not responding to God's initiative will, in their becoming, begin to pull further away from the dreams and values of God until they have lost sight of them entirely; and thus, over a period of time, the "gap" between heaven and hell may widen.

Hell does not seem to be a possibility "outside" of God, for nothing, even hell, can exist without God. Hell seems to be a state or condition in which some beings will exist, wherein they will be totally unaware of and insensitive to any good. They have divorced themselves from God's stimulation and will apparently continue not only to be unaware of God but also to lose sight of anything meaningful in life and so exist in the state called "hell."

Sin or evil may be like an infection our bodies get periodically that slows down the activity of our bodies but will never stop it. Those responding to God's initiative are like white blood cells. They, by their very existence, are combating infection and bringing in health, or the coming of God's kingdom. Infection (unresponsive persons) will either be cleared up (forgiveness and healing) or sealed off (hell). In its extreme, a being totally unresponsive to God slips into a state where it remains in apathy and negativism.

The world may be seen to be like a flowing energy system. Sin or evil obstructs this system and thus causes all sorts of reactions and negative interactions within the entities living in the scope of its influence. The activity of God in the coming of his kingdom is bringing a wholeness and coherence back into the "system" wherein an immunity is building up in an ever-increasing degree and will some day contain the infection. Hell is the contained infection. God's activity in achieving this seems to be in both general and specific events. The general events would be the things involved in the kingdom of heaven growing like a seed (Matthew 13:24-30). The specific events would be happenings like the Second Coming (1 Corinthians 15:51-57).

God's judgment may be likened to his acceptance of the condition of entities unresponsive to him over the ages. He allows them to isolate themselves and will accept them or grant them existence in their isolated and cutoff state. They will apparently ever remain in that state.

The ideas and concepts in this chapter give me a possible framework in which to relate the gospel, the things occurring in the field of parapsychology, what I know about science, physics, and other fields. They are possibilities that make sense to me and have been helpful to others. The Good News remains the same, but it can be told in so many different ways. The Holy Spirit, I believe, wants us to expand our concepts of God and the way he is working. We need to be creative and innovative. As long as there is faithfulness to the message of God, we should feel free to express it in ever-increasing new ways.

There are many things that can be considered from this chapter. Are there statements, for example, in this chapter that could not be considered to be Christian from your point of view? Do you see the universe as a whole? Do you think of all things being or existing because of God's presence in them? Can anything exist separate from God? Do you conceive of yourself more in an individual way or as a part of a larger whole? How do you react to the suggestions considering a continuance of life perspective? Does it bother you to think of more than one earth experience? Why? What is your conception of the kingdom of heaven?

Chapter VI

NEW THOUGHTS
ABOUT
THE MIND

This last chapter brings us to discuss what I feel may be the most practical subject to everyone who reads and encounters this material. This chapter deals with the mind or our center of thought. I include it because parapsychology is finding the mind to be so potentially powerful. Psychics seem to be able to focus their minds or to concentrate with intense control. The results, as shown in some of the phenomena, even to the extent of moving matter, are causing us to question the extent of our mental potential. There is a lot to think about, therefore, in this area.

I have basically pictured an entity (person or being) as consisting of that which seems to be God's image also, as having form, spirit or energy, and mind (or thought). We know a lot about our physiologies. This is the aspect of ourselves that is the most concrete and most easily studied, for our five senses can be overtly involved in its discovery. The energy aspect of ourselves is just being discovered, and empirical data are being analyzed, organized, and categorized all the time. It will probably not take too many years for us to be able to be as aware of the bioplasma body as we are of our physical bodies. We will be using this aspect of our reality for many different benefits—from observing the auras of plants for weather prediction to understanding more the oneness of all life. We will thus gain practical and philosophical benefit. When we realize that to violate any life is to violate one's own life and all life, we may have a better world. I look forward to the time when the information about this energy or spirit aspect of ourselves is as advanced as that of our physiology. We are probably just in the infancy stage now.

It does not seem to me that we are as yet really beginning to understand fully the mind or thoughts, but we are seeing more all the time of what the mind can do. The mind is powerful; it seems to be the center of our being. The mind is that from which thoughts emanate. It is the aspect of ourselves that possibly even "creates our own being." That is a strong statement, and I will speak more about it later. The mind is not the brain. The brain is a part of our "earth suit"; and as soon as one terminates life in that physical body, the mind moves out. The mind seems to be the awareness center of our being. Whether the mind and the energy body are ineluctably intertwined, we don't know. When one dies, the energy aspect of one's reality is seen "floating free" from the body. The mind must be a part of that, but whether it is "in" that has yet to be determined.

Thoughts May Create

The mind creates thought, and the thought it creates seems to remain a part of it. That is, one's thoughts are the outreaches of one's mind, and one seems *always* to be connected to one's thoughts. All our thoughts are a part of us and may exist as a present part of our being. Our minds may be the total of all our thoughts; so as we think, so is the size, shape, and content of our minds. The mind may be ever-growing, ever-expanding, and the growing and expanding may be the basic core of what we are.

If entities are the accumulation of their past thoughts and their present thinking, there is probably the widest divergence of all between different beings in this area of our reality. These things cannot be proven, of course, but there always has to be a theoretical framework from which we work. Let us say, then, that one's mind is the center of one's being and, as with God, is the basic substance of one's being. (Albert Einstein was convinced matter was just a condensed form of energy. Energy may be just a condensed form of thought.) The changing progress of this basic substance would be from mind to energy to form, all different states of the basic substance. If we would reverse the order, then we would move from our physical bodies, which we leave, to our energy bodies (which we don't know if we leave), to our mind reality or thoughts.

God the Father, the mind reality of God, seems to have created all that exists by his thoughts literally shaping what he conceptualized. "They deliberately ignore this fact, that by the word of God heavens existed long ago" (2 Peter 3:5). If this is the way God called things into being, might this also be true with us? Do we create, shape, rework, and build reality by our thoughts? If we do, it will be one of the most fantastic discoveries yet about ourselves as "beings," and it will make all other awarenesses seem like child's play compared with the ramifications of this possibility. I believe, by the way, that this may very well be true: we do create, shape, rework, and build reality by our thoughts. I also believe the Bible teaches this truth, that Jesus was aware of it, and that "faith" is explained or understood because of this truth. I hope to be able to show the reader how it is possible, for if it is true, it is a very important discovery for one to make.

The Power of the Mind

I don't have to build a case to show that the mind is more powerful than we ever realized. The whole field of parapsychology is pointing to the mind, especially telepathy, PK, thoughtography, etc. All are shouting out: "The mind is amazing, and more powerful than we ever imagined!" Leslie Weatherhead said several years ago that the power of the mind over the body is so immense it is hard to find where the line of limitation might run. He added that it is difficult to know what cannot be achieved if the necessary physical apparatus is there.[1]

The mind develops thoughts that exist as reality, that move out to be a force in themselves to bring what is imagined into being. Thoughts, or the mind, move and seem to direct the energy body. Thoughts move and direct the physical body. Thoughts may think into being and think out of being. Psychologically we know thoughts can cause a condition conducive to illness. They can make one feel ill when one's physiology is not ill until the physiology even develops the symptoms of that imagined illness. We are talking about an important aspect of a physician's awareness that some patients have psychosomatic illnesses. These are patients who are not really physically ill, but who think they are. If they think so long enough, they can actually "cause it to happen." These are also patients with real illnesses and diseases that were "allowed to develop" because of the patients' mental state.

We will some day possibly prove that our physical bodies have within them a built-in perpetual health-creation and maintenance system that functions erroneously because of its being tampered with by the mind of the user. Worry, fear, hate, jealousy, anxiety, and a host of other traits have powerful negative effects on our bodies, both physical and energy. There are many diseases doctors are calling "stress" diseases. These illnesses are caused by or aggravated by stress. Stress affects the digestive system, nervous system, muscle-joint functioning, and circulatory system, and it causes allergic disorders, etc. Stress is a condition of the body which the mind has permitted to develop. Through our discoveries with mind control we are learning how to teach the aspect of psychosomatic health. If one's mind can cause all sorts of illnesses, why can't it cause or create a condition for better resilience and continued health? It can, and it does.

I have not mentioned hypnosis (other than just referring to it as an alternate consciousness state) in any of the previous pages because I have not been quite sure how to categorize it. I mention it here because it shows and demonstrates the tremendous capabilities of thought or belief. Hypnosis is a state of mind persons who are hypnotized allow themselves to be in. One cannot usually hypnotize persons who are determined not to be hypnotized. Hypnosis is done with the permission of the subjects, whose minds move into a state wherein they allow the hypnotist to direct their thinking. We still do not know exactly how it works, but we do see what happens as it works.

Just a couple of months ago I watched a group of college young people up on chairs screaming because the floor was covered with mice; unable to count the fingers on their hands; unable to speak without stuttering profusely; unable to put on their shoes, and when they did, putting them on the wrong feet. All of this was due to the suggestions of a professional hypnotist who was the assembly speaker that day. What their minds believed, they saw, felt, tasted, and experienced. What a person believes to be true becomes true, to that person.

There are some good books available for information about hypnosis and the theories behind it. I don't wish to get into this area in detail. I mention it because, under hypnosis, a person can perform feats normally thought impossible. Lew March was the hypnotist who gave the program at Merced College. He weighs about 160 pounds. I watched him take a girl who was hypnotized and who weighed about 92 pounds, place her on two chairs with her head on one and her feet on the other—she was stiff as a board—and then stand on her midsection. She seemed to feel nothing afterward. Under hypnosis persons can perform amazing physical and mental feats because they *believe* they can. They have no question about being able to do them since the one they have allowed to hypnotize them says they can or can't, and thus it happens that way.

Maxwell Maltz in *Psycho-Cybernetics* says a lot about this particular idea. He mentions in his book that creative imagination enters into every act. He sees imagination as picturing our goals; then our bodies act to fulfill these goals. He thinks we act because of imagination, not because of "will," as most people think. Persons act and feel according to what they imagine is true about themselves in relationship to their environment. He also believes the nervous system cannot tell the imagined and the real experience apart. Your nervous system reacts to the imagined and the real the same way therefore. He points out that when the hypnotist has guided the subject to the point where he is convinced that what the hypnotist says is true, the subject then behaves differently, for he thinks and believes differently. Maltz believes one acts and feels according to how his mind imagines things to be, not according to what they really are like. He further states his opinion that everyone is to some degree hypnotized, either by ideas he has uncritically accepted from others, or by ideas he has persuaded himself are true.[2]

John Lilly brings another concept into this discussion. He feels that the "limits of one's beliefs set the limits of the experiences." He says, "I realized that where I had been at each stage of my life was determined by my beliefs at that time."[3]

What tremendous implications this awareness has! What our minds believe sets up what we see, experience, and expect. As persons believe, so are they. What persons believe they can or cannot do is what they evidence.

Some people call what persons believe themselves to be "having a life script." This leads to what may be called "script analysis." Eric Berne is considered the father of these ideas, as they are developed in his book *Games People Play*. The concept is that we all in our minds write our own life scripts. Our belief frameworks determine what we expect we can or can't do in life. We know this is true in the sense that we live according to our own expectations (which are often really others' expectations). A life-script counselor would work to help us evaluate the scripts we have written for ourselves and rewrite them for more fulfilling lives.

A life script proceeds from a "self image." That is, from our own image of ourselves we write our own life scripts. Or, proceeding from what we think we can do, we mentally plan our own future. Maxwell Maltz considers the discovery of the "self image" to be the most important discovery of this century. He suggests we all carry around with us a blueprint picture of ourselves that is the conception we have of ourselves as the sort of persons we are. This conception has come from what we believe about ourselves, and that has come from our past experiences. All the successes and failures of the past, particularly those of our childhoods, have pulled together to give us the experiences that have formed the beliefs from which emanate our self-concept. Once the picture we have of ourselves is completed, it becomes "true," as far as one is personally concerned. He says one does not question the validity but proceeds to act upon it just as if it were true. He pins the importance of the self image down to two important things: (1) All one's actions, feelings, behavior, and even abilities are always consistent with this self image. (2) The self image can be changed.[4]

This concept of how the person is comprised is the major therapeutic construct from which some therapists work. Maltz goes on to say that a person's self image is the key to his/her personality and behavior. He thinks that self-image psychology, which has been proved by its merits, explains many phenomena which have not yet been properly understood. He refers to the following types of personalities: "success-type," "happiness" and "unhappiness-prone," "health-prone" and "disease-prone." In his opinion, self-image psychology helps us to understand more about these personality types as well as other things we observe in personalities. It also explains how positive thinking works and why it works, and why it works with some and not with others. Positive thinking works if the self image is consistent with that philosophy, or if the self image is acceptable to the idea that things can look positive.[5]

There are many "positive thinking" books and courses. These exist because positive thinking has worked for a lot of people. Those who believe in the concept of positive thinking believe that the way they look at things, or think about situations, can make a difference. Persons mentally create their own success or failure because they function according to their thoughts. This again speaks about persons fulfilling their own expectations, or seeing what they wish to see, or being what they wish to be, by beginning to "see" themselves as they wish to be. Auto-hypnosis or self-hypnosis teaches persons to set up an imagery system that will draw them into a success and achievement pattern instead of a failure one.

Three Aspects of the Mind

The mind seems to have three different aspects to it. They can be distinguished as the conscious mind or the conscious part of the mind, the subconscious part of the mind, and a higher or superconscious part of the mind. I trust that the following conceptualization of how our minds may work will clarify the brief statement and will be beneficial to the reader.

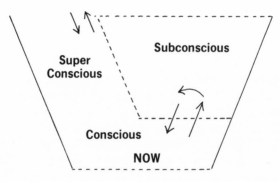

I think that this way of looking at the mind can provide a framework for understanding what parapsychologists and others before them have been discussing about the mind and thoughts. I want to suggest the possible relationship between these three aspects of the mind.

The conscious seems to interact with life. What it experiences feeds into the subconscious where everything goes (the accumulation of all the "now" experiences), and during the sleeping periods the higher conscious seeks to intergrate it all together in a functional and satisfactory manner. This would fit into the statement of Stanley Krippner when he said that everyone dreams. Some remember the dreams while others do not. He indicates that if someone is prevented from dreaming over a long period of time, the consequences can be severe—even to the point of hallucinating in the waking state.[6] We need to give our higher or superconscious time to "help us out."

The superconscious aspect of one's mind is the part of the mind that may be seen as a "higher self," reaching out for the best for one's self. This is where God's initiative and stimulation are experienced. This part of our consciousness is open to that which is beyond ourselves, whether seen as open to God or as related to the "collective unconscious" to which Carl Jung refers.[7] Part is probably collective in humanity and part is above that, as God's stimulative thoughts.

From this area come our dreams, visions, hopes, and anticipations if we are open to them. The desire for meaning, purpose, and happiness comes from here. Everyone, deep within, has the desire to love and be loved, to feel worthwhile to one's self and others. This comes from the higher self that seeks to "nudge" persons to enter into experiences conducive to their finest development. From this aspect of our minds come the dreams for peace, oneness, and unity. Even though humankind cannot find peace, we can conceptualize it. It is this conceptualization that keeps us reaching toward it. If we could remain fully open to this aspect of our mental reality, we would probably remain in our most creative state and eventually find our goals reached.

The conscious aspect of our minds might be designated as the mind's cutting edge. This is the direct present conscious level of our state. This is where we are right now. In our becoming we are shaped or formed by living experiences. The conscious level is the present experience of our choosing and living. It is on the conscious level that we think, evaluate, and change. It is on this level that we experience the intention of our own selves. There are all sorts of influences coming at us from all around, from friends, society, and our higher selves. The conscious mind, though, is the state of our current being. The consciousness on this level can change the whole pattern of our being by its choosing to remain the same, to regress, or to move ahead.

I put the subconscious aspect last because it seems to be the total of all the entity's experiences, patterns, or accumulations up to that point. The subconscious may be the learned patterns to that point that are habitual or what will happen automatically if nothing intentional is occurring. If persons are not acting with intention consciously, they are acting from habit or learned patterns subconsciously. The subconscious might be likened to a memory bank that has accumulated everything a person is up to that point, from which we develop a "self concept" and write our life scripts.

What is important to realize here is that if we are acting unintentionally, we will be simply following past patterns. To the degree we act thoughtfully and intentionally, we can change in our becoming. If we do not use our minds consciously, in creativity, independence, thoughtful evaluation, analysis, etc., we will just go along as before. To the degree that we interact consciously with our living, we will restructure and reshape it. As enough new conscious material feeds in, the self-concept will be in a process of change and development.

The natural acting out of our living seems to be from the subconscious. When we are "not thinking," we are fulfilling subconscious thought patterns. When we are thinking, we are creating new thought patterns and are in the process of reforming the subconscious and thus the self-concept. Positive thinking creates new thought patterns that cause a juggling around in the subconscious that begins a changed self-concept. The rate that new material is fed into the subconscious (through conscious activity) is the rate that the self-concept can change. In other words the harder one works at it, the faster it will occur.

Faith

We are faith living when our conscious, rather than just following the subconscious, moves to be open to our higher conscious and thus launches out to believe and look for that which is beyond our selves. Faith takes us beyond our selves. It taps into the impossible and hears it is possible. The superconscious realizes the potential of our being and would lead us to seek it even though it is not yet consciously visible. It allows us to move beyond what we have been conditioned to believe we can become.

The two "pulls" are from the subconscious on one side that says what we can do is what we always have done and always have thought ourselves to be, and the higher self or superconscious that says there are no limits to what we can do and who we can become. Faith is following the higher calling. What limits our becoming is being contained within the traditional thought patterns of the subconscious. If new programming is given the subconscious (as can be done in hypnosis), then new achievement, belief, and direction can be attained. Faith, though, may be a better way.

If we open up in faith to the leading of God in our higher selves, and if we follow that leading, there are no limits to our becoming. Faith transcends the limiting feelings that originate from the traditional expectation patterns of the subconscious. The way of becoming through faith would be for the superconscious to be continually open to God as it feeds stimulation to the conscious aspect of the mind. The consciousness of our selves moves out believing and will be continually amazed at what occurs as it feeds ever new material into the subconscious for the continuous reshaping and renewing of that aspect of our minds. (This can be seen visually in the diagram on page 99.)

Hypnosis is the method used by some therapists that helps persons change themselves, by the reprogramming of the subconscious, to provide a different belief framework for the effect of the subconscious on the conscious until the clients open themselves up to their higher potentials. This might be seen as priming the belief or change pump until the higher self takes over on its own. If these persons do not consciously wish to change, they may exist in a rather stagnant and uninteresting pattern for many years, which would be the complacent recycling of the conscious, simply acting out the patterns of the subconscious and thus the conscious never feeding anything new into the subconscious for its changing.

Thinking into Being

I want to move further into areas related to the creative power of the mind. In this emphasis I wish to augment the possibility that our thoughts are a force that actually create their intent. We know this is true in terms of persons with themselves but to conceive of it as being true related to phenomena outside of our selves may be a new idea to many.

Carl Jung seemed to have noticed how we were completely overlooking the possibility of the reality of thoughts. He sees it a paradox that we do not think·that a thought is a reality so we treat it as nothing. Even if we think the thought is true, we feel that it exists only because it represents certain facts. Jung uses the example of the atom bomb to demonstrate the absurdity of our thinking here. We can produce a devastating fact like the atom bomb but yet not establish the reality of the thought itself.[8] He also uses the discovery of J. B. Rhine, that the attitudes of the researcher and the subject have an effect on the outcome of the parapsychological experiment. This indicates the influence of thought and mind attitude on the project: thoughts may be real "things" indeed.[9]

William Tiller, from Stanford University, has entertained the possibility that by projecting a suitable thought pattern with one's mind, one can create a force that generates a set of waves that interact with basic wave components and can thus change the basic wave patterns. He clearly seems to believe we are discovering the fact that thoughts can alter occurrences.[10] Dr. Edgar Mitchell says that as the particle physicists continue to explore atomic and subatomic structures, they are discovering that the thoughts and intentions of observers may be a real influence in the experiments. In other words, the thoughts of the observers are affecting the experiment. He also states:

> ... at the point of the mind one can bring about changes in the organization of structure in the various levels of some substances. That is, through mind forces one can create a pattern, and that pattern then acts as a force field which applies to the next level of substance.[11]

Our minds may create patterns that affect certain substances that are affected by thought patterns. The substances that thought affected then move on in the sequencing of different consequential steps to influence other substances that thought cannot directly affect. Let's say that thoughts could move some tiny grains of sand that would free a rock to roll and hit a larger rock, dislodging it to knock loose a boulder. Our minds have the power to move things that can move things, to achieve what we believe will happen.

To concentrate on something happening might begin a series of happenings that might eventually bring to fruition that which we hope for. Things that take very little juggling to occur could possibly happen quite soon. Things that take a lot of effecting to occur would necessarily happen over a longer period of time. This may explain why some prayers are answered immediately while others are fulfilled over extended periods of time.

I'm suggesting the possibility that faith is a force in itself that joins with God in causing something to happen. If this is true, it is indeed an essential aspect of something occurring, even as the Scriptures indicate. Believers may be an actual part of creating the framework for the answer to their own prayers. Faith may be an actual force in itself—that is, really a mind framework—that moves to answer one's own prayers. The belief that it can happen—that God wants it to happen—releases thought forces that may begin creating the very framework for its happening.

This would not take God "out of the picture," as some might feel. It makes what God has created a part of what it becomes. It means that faith is not just an attitude toward God but also a condition of the one seeking God. The stronger one's faith, the stronger the force that is released to bring the result. Looking to God, believing he will bring something about, and knowing he will respond releases or turns loose from the seeker a source from within the believer that God has put there, for the actual creation of that hoped for. Hebrews 11:1 says, "Now faith is the assurance of things hoped for, the conviction of things not seen." As we come to God in faith, God opens up within us an aspect of ourselves that possibly makes us (the believers) the channel for the achievement of our own seeking.

We find that the concept of thoughts being a thing in themselves—a force that actually moves out—is again a phenomenon set up in the way God has made things that can be used for good or for evil. Positive thinkers claim that positive thinking works for anyone if the person applies its principles consistently. The mind, as the creator of many of our situations, seems to be attested to by many, whether God is consciously involved or not.

From our Christian viewpoint, Jesus was very clear in stating that nothing is impossible if one believes hard enough. Matthew 21:21-22 says:

> And Jesus answered them, "Truly, I say to you, if you have faith and never doubt, you will not only do what has been done to the fig tree, but even if you say to this mountain, 'Be taken up and cast into the sea,' it will be done. And whatever you ask in prayer, you will receive, if you have faith."

Jesus' two illustrations in these verses are significant to me, for both seemed like rather senseless things to do with faith. Jesus was passing a fig tree that was barren, and the disciples were with him. Because it had no fruit, he spoke to it, saying it would never bear fruit again. It withered before the eyes of the disciples. Why would one wish to do that, and why would one wish to move a mountain? The two examples that seem rather ridiculous put before us the picture that faith can achieve anything, not because the something is that important, but because it puts to work certain happenings from one's mind or thoughts that cause its occurrence. In a sense, I think Jesus was saying that if you realized the potential of your minds, and if you wanted something strongly enough and believed it would happen, then certain phenomena would begin to occur that would bring it to fruition. In the context of faith, anything can be done for God if you believe.

The concept of thoughts being real things that emanate from the mind, which seems to be the center of one's being, could fit into the concept in Genesis of the spoken word being the process of creation. Words are thoughts, or they represent thoughts. Maybe God's thoughts became words, that became energy, that became the matter that accomplished his dreams. Who knows? Maybe we will someday not think it strange at all to conceive of thinking or speaking something into existence. Maybe the "Word" refers both to Christ and to the method of its occurrence.

There are some stories of psychics who are able to materialize and dematerialize certain objects. Some of these seem to be in fairly closely observed situations, but I do not know of any sound empirical evidence in support of the claims. I don't think it is out of the question, though, if our suggestions are within the framework of possibility. In my cosmological treatment of God I discussed the possibility that the Father was the mental aspect of God, and that from him, or from his thought, came all other realities. I think the pattern is thought, to energy, to matter or form. If this progression is accurate, then thought would be the basic causative factor in both the resulting phenomena.

The emphasis in the Scripture on both one's thoughts and the words one speaks leaves me with the impression that what I have been presenting as a possibility is occurring. Matthew 12:36 states:

> "I tell you, on the day of judgment men will render account for every careless word they utter; for by your words you will be justified, and by your words you will be condemned."

Why? Possibly because your words emanate from your thoughts and your thoughts are you. I mentioned in the first part of this chapter that all one's thoughts are possibly an extension of one's self and thus are always a part of one's self. We think that because we forget something, it is gone. However, it is apparently still with us and always will be. When Jesus indicates we will be judged for every word, even the meaningless ones, he may simply be recognizing the truth that we never lose any thought aspects of ourselves, because they are ourselves. Forgiveness may thus not refer to the "forgetting" of past thoughts as much as the positive overpowering of new thoughts that supercede the others.

It's All in the Mind

The battle of life seems to be in the mind. That is where it appears to be won or lost. Much of our reality may proceed from our minds, and what we think about may be creating what occurs; whether it occurs objectively in the objective circumstance is not as important as realizing it occurs from the perspective of the one who believes it. For example, if a person is worried sick about something that might occur, the worry takes its toll on the worrier whether it happens or not. If it never actually occurs, it can really occur in the mind and emotions of the worrier.

Persons can think "sick" or think "well," see the beautiful and alive, or see the ugly and decaying. We can look at bees and see honey or a stinger, look at roses and see a lovely flower or thorns. The most important aspect of this seems to be that if we see only stingers, thorns, etc., that is what there will be for us. If we see beauty, honey, or flowers, that is what will be there. Our minds create the world we see and live in. We live in a world that is neutral, that is, colorless, without interpretation. Interpretation brings it to life, making it the most marvelous or the worst place in the world. Being a saint or a sinner appears to be an "inside" job.

Persons negative against God and life have let their minds become thus. Genesis 6:5 says: "The Lord saw that the wickedness of man was great in the earth, and that every imagination of the thoughts of his heart was only evil continually." Romans 1:21 says: "For although they knew God they did not honor him as God or give thanks to him, but they became futile in their thinking and their senseless minds were darkened."

The condition of what the apostle Paul calls the "carnal mind" or the "spiritual mind" seems to be determined in the mind. Romans 8:6 states: "To set the mind on the flesh is death, but to set the mind on the Spirit is life and peace." I would like to interpret it another way: To let your thoughts exist on the level of decaying negative life is to kill your own mind, but to let your thoughts exist on the level of the beauty of life in God is to bring to your mind peace and aliveness to your living. Jesus clearly articulates this truth in Mark 7:20-22:

> . . . "What comes out of a man is what defiles a man. For from within, out of the heart of man, come evil thoughts, fornication, theft, murder, adultery, coveting, wickedness, deceit, licentiousness, envy, slander, pride, foolishness."

Titus 1:15 puts it succinctly:

> A person who is pure of heart sees goodness and purity in everything; but a person whose own heart is evil and untrustworthy finds evil in everything,

for his dirty mind and rebellious heart color all he sees and hears (author's translation).

The sobering thought about this whole thing is that what we allow ourselves to think is what we are creating for ourselves, what we are becoming. If a church gives way to gossip and negativism, it will become that. If a country does so, it will also reap from itself the thoughts of itself. We all seem to reap from ourselves the thoughts of ourselves. In Proverbs, Solomon makes a powerful statement about this truth (4:20-21):

> Listen, son of mine, to what I say. Listen carefully and keep these thoughts ever in mind; let them penetrate deep within your heart, for they will mean real life to you, and radiant health (author's translation).

Solomon seemed to be aware that to keep one's thoughts on the right track brought peace from the thoughts themselves and a healthy future the thoughts were creating.

Of all the things we have covered that in some way relate to para-psychological phenomena and the Christian faith, this is probably the most practical, for everyone of us has his or her own thought life or thought world. I would like to end this material, therefore, with some suggestions for making our world, as Christians, a very meaningful one. Each suggestion in itself could be a book:

1. We need to try to keep in mind that our thoughts are forming us; we are becoming what we are thinking.

2. We can learn to control our thinking, direct it.

3. We can search for the good and beautiful in everything. Our concentration on the beautiful may keep our concentration off the negative.

4. We should never allow ourselves to hate or to despise. As soon as we do, the one we hate seems to take us over. When Jesus said to love your enemies, he was probably thinking about the one who should love. He knew that when we hate, we begin to destroy ourselves.

5. We can learn to relax and enjoy life.

6. If something is frustrating any one of us, we might ask ourselves if it is worth it and make adjustments if it is not.

7. We should establish priorities for our living according to our real values. We can evaluate whether these primary values are way down the list in the use of our time or not.

8. We can continue to look long range as to whether what is upsetting us now will really matter in a few years.

9. We can continually seek God.

God has created a universe wherein what he has made continues to be involved in its own shaping and becoming. This realization is both sobering and exciting.

Every new discovery leads to even newer discoveries. For example, really learning about our physical bodies leads to the awareness of the things that are unexplainable from just a physiological viewpoint. The more we know about our physical bodies, the more we know we are more than just that. The more we are learning about our energy bodies, the more we are recognizing that this awareness does not explain everything about us either; so now we move on to the mind, or the power of thoughts. Where do we go from there?

I hope that the intentions indicated for this book have been realized: (1) to help you be more aware of the things occurring in the field of parapsychology; (2) to help you think through where you are in openness to things happening today; (3) to show you some of the ways I have come to look at the phenomena occurring; and (4) to encourage you to follow your own "becoming" without holding back because others may not be at that same place, too.

As you discuss this chapter, you might examine what you traditionally felt about the mind. Have you thought of your "thinking" being separate from your self? Is it conceivable to you that you might have a real part in the answering of your own prayers? Does the concept that faith may be one's joining with God to cause something to happen take away from God? Do you find it difficult to accept the possibility that what you think is who you are and what you are becoming?

NOTES

Chapter I

[1] "Psychic Research: A New Awareness," *California Living,* weekly magazine of the *San Francisco Examiner and Chronicle,* July 1, 1973.

[2] *Psychic,* July, 1973, p. 50.

[3] *Ibid.*

[4] *Ibid.*

[5] Alvin Toffler, *Future Shock* (New York: Random House, Inc., 1970), p. 398.

[6] "Perspective," *Trends; A Journal of Resources,* May/June, 1970, p. 1.

[7] Richard H. Neff, *Psychic Phenomena and Religion* (Philadelphia: The Westminster Press, 1971), p. 11.

[8] *Ibid.,* p. 17.

[9] Robert E. Ornstein, *The Psychology of Consciousness* (San Francisco: W. H. Freeman and Company, 1972), pp. 99, 181, 184-185.

[10] J. B. Rhine, *The Reach of the Mind* (New York: William Sloane Associates, Inc., 1947), p. 206.

[11] J. B. Rhine, *New World of the Mind* (New York: William Sloane Associates, Inc., 1953), p. 195.

[12] *Ibid.,* p. 150.

[13] Joseph Campbell, ed., *The Portable Jung,* trans. R.F.C. Hull (New York: The Viking Press, Inc., 1971), p. 481.

[14] Claudio Naranjo, *The One Quest* (New York: The Viking Press, Inc., 1972), p. 35.

[15] *Ibid.,* p. 78.

[16] Neff, *Psychic Phenomena and Religion,* p. 49.

[17] Stanford University, *The Dimensions of Healing,* Symposium, Sept. 30–Oct. 4, 1972 (Los Altos, Calif.: Academy of Parapsychology and Medicine, n.d.).

[18] *Trends,* May/June, 1970.

Chapter II

[1] Michael Murphy, "I Experienced a Kind of Clarity," *Intellectual Digest*, January, 1973, p. 20.

[2] Gardner Murphy in Montague Ullman, Stanley Krippner, and Alan Vaughan, *Dream Telepathy* (New York: Macmillan Publishing Co., Inc., 1973), p. vii.

[3] *Ibid.*, p. 227.

[4] *Ibid.*, p. 224.

[5] Robert E. Ornstein, *The Psychology of Consciousness* (San Francisco: W. H. Freeman and Company, 1972), p. 150.

[6] Andrew Weil, *The Natural Mind* (Boston: Houghton Mifflin Company, 1972), pp. 34-35.

[7] John C. Lilly, *The Center of the Cyclone* (New York: The Julian Press, 1972), p. 3.

[8] Weil, *The Natural Mind*, p. 19.

[9] *Ibid.*, p. 195.

[10] Carlos Castaneda, *The Teachings of Don Juan: A Yaqui Way of Knowledge* (New York: Ballantine Books, 1968), *passim*.

[11] Weil, *The Natural Mind*, p. 194.

[12] Lilly, *The Center of the Cyclone*, pp. 75, 76.

[13] Ornstein, *The Psychology of Consciousness*, p. 7.

[14] *Ibid.*, pp. 104, 107.

[15] Leslie D. Weatherhead, *Psychology, Religion and Healing*, rev. ed. (Nashville: Abingdon Press, 1951), pp. 215-216.

[16] Ornstein, *The Psychology of Consciousness*, p. 108.

[17] Paul Chance, "Parapsychology Is an Idea Whose Time Has Come," *Psychology Today*, October, 1973, pp. 116, 120.

[18] Sheila Ostrander and Lynn Schroeder, *Psychic Discoveries Behind the Iron Curtain* (Englewood Cliffs, N.J.: Prentice-Hall, Inc., 1970), pp. 77-78.

[19] *Ibid.*, pp. 357-361.

[20] Ron Caylor, "America's Largest Nursing School Is Now Teaching Psychic Healing," *National Enquirer*, March 24, 1974.

[21] *Ibid.*

[22] Ostrander and Schroeder, *Psychic Discoveries*, pp. 158-160.

[23] *Ibid.*, p. 166.

[24] "The Theory of Acupuncture," *Intellectual Digest*, September, 1973, p. 21.

[25] "Using Acupuncture As a Substitute for Novocaine," *San Francisco Chronicle*, April 9, 1973, p. 3.

[26] Ostrander and Schroeder, *Psychic Discoveries*, pp. 331-333.

[27] Douglas Dean, "I Witnessed Startling Advances in Russian ESP Research," *National Enquirer*, September 24, 1972.

Chapter III

[1] Stanford University, *The Dimensions of Healing* (Los Altos, Calif.: Academy of Parapsychology and Medicine, n.d.), p. 21.

[2] Douglas Dean, "I Witnessed Startling Advances in Russian ESP Research," *National Enquirer*, Sept. 24, 1972.

[3] *Ibid.*

[4] Stanford University, *The Dimensions of Healing*, pp. 29-34.

[5] *Ibid.*, pp. 121-131.

[6] Ron Caylor, "America's Largest Nursing School Is Now Teaching Psychic Healing," *National Enquirer*, March 24, 1974.

[7] Douglas Dean, "I Witnessed Startling Advances in Russian ESP Research," *National Enquirer,* Sept. 24, 1972.

[8] Joseph Banks Rhine, *The Reach of the Mind* (New York: William Sloane Associates, Inc., 1947), p. 217.

Chapter IV

[1] Norma Lee Browning, *The Psychic World of Peter Hurkos* (New York: Doubleday & Company, Inc., 1970), pp. 114, 204-212, 241.

[2] Charles Petit, "Philippines' Psychic Healer 'Dr. Tony,'" *San Francisco Chronicle,* June 25, 1973, p. 2.

[3] "Interview with Harold Sherman," *Psychic,* February, 1974, p. 37.

[4] Ruth Montgomery, *A World Beyond* (New York: Coward, McCann & Geoghegan, Inc., 1971), p. 7.

[5] Richard H. Neff, *Psychic Phenomena and Religion* (Philadelphia: The Westminster Press, 1971), pp. 51, 66.

[6] Robert E. Ornstein, *The Psychology of Consciousness* (San Francisco: W. H. Freeman and Company, 1972), p. 82.

[7] Neff, *Psychic Phenomena and Religion,* p. 131.

Chapter V

[1] Stanford University, *The Dimensions of Healing* (Los Altos, Calif.: Academy of Parapsychology and Medicine, n.d.), p. 7.

[2] "The Princeton Galaxy," *Intellectual Digest,* June, 1973, p. 29.

[3] *Ibid.*

[4] Stanford University, *The Dimensions of Healing,* p. 24.

[5] John C. Lilly, *The Center of the Cyclone* (New York: The Julian Press, 1972), p. 204.

[6] Claudio Naranjo, *The One Quest* (New York: The Viking Press, Inc., 1972), p. 138.

[7] Joseph Campbell, ed., *The Portable Jung,* trans R. F. C. Hull (New York: The Viking Press, Inc., 1972), p. 470.

[8] Quincy Howe, Jr., *Reincarnation for the Christian* (Philadelphia: The Westminster Press, 1974), p. 24.

[9] Naranjo, *The One Quest,* p. 137.

[10] Montague Ullman, Stanley Krippner, and Alan Vaughan, *Dream Telepathy* (New York: Macmillan Publishing Co., Inc., 1973), p. 227.

[11] Robert E. Ornstein, *The Psychology of Consciousness* (San Francisco: W. H. Freeman and Company, 1972), p. 20.

[12] John B. Cobb, Jr., *A Christian Natural Theology* (Philadelphia: The Westminster Press, 1965), p. 56.

[13] Stanford University, *The Dimensions of Healing,* pp. 151, 152.

[14] Curt John Ducasse, *The Belief in a Life After Death* (Springfield, Ill.: Charles C. Thomas, 1961), p. 213.

[15] Howe, *Reincarnation for the Christian,* pp. 82-83.

[16] *Ibid.,* p. 11.

[17] *Ibid.,* p. 13.

[18] *Ibid.,* pp. 30-31.

[19] *Ibid.,* p. 48.

Chapter VI

[1] Leslie Weatherhead, *Psychology, Religion and Healing* (Nashville: Abingdon Press, 1951), p. 111.

[2] Maxwell Maltz, *Psycho-Cybernetics* (Englewood Cliffs, N.J.: Prentice-Hall, Inc., 1971), pp. 28, 29, 31, 49-51.

[3] John C. Lilly, *The Center of the Cyclone* (New York: The Julian Press, 1972), pp. 17, 18.

[4] Maltz, *Psycho-Cybernetics,* pp. 2-3.

[5] *Ibid.,* p. ix.

[6] Montague Ullman, Stanley Krippner, and Alan Vaughan, *Dream Telepathy* (New York: Macmillan Publishing Co., Inc., 1973), p. 76.

[7] Joseph Campbell, ed., *The Portable Jung,* trans. R.F.C. Hull (New York: The Viking Press, Inc., 1971), p. 34.

[8] *Ibid.,* p. 486.

[9] *Ibid.,* p. 510.

[10] Stanford University. *The Dimensions of Healing* (Los Altos, Calif.: Academy of Parapsychology and Medicine, n.d.), p. 68.

[11] *California Living,* weekly magazine of the *San Francisco Examiner and Chronicle,* July 1, 1973.

BIBLIOGRAPHY

Books

Browning, Norma Lee, *The Psychic World of Peter Hurkos.* Garden City, N.Y.: Doubleday & Company, Inc., 1970.

Campbell, Joseph, ed., *The Portable Jung.* Trans. R.F.C. Hull. New York: The Viking Press, Inc., 1971.

Caprio, Frank S., and Berger, Joseph R., *Helping Yourself with Self-Hypnosis.* Englewood Cliffs, N.J.: Prentice-Hall, Inc., 1963.

Castenada, Carlos, *Journey to Ixtlan.* New York: Simon & Schuster, Inc., 1972.

_____, *A Separate Reality.* New York: Simon & Schuster, Inc., 1971.

_____, *The Teachings of Don Juan: A Yaqui Way of Knowledge.* New York: Ballantine Books, Inc., 1968.

Cobb, John B., Jr., *A Christian Natural Theology.* Philadelphia: The Westminster Press, 1965.

Dane, Christopher, *Psychic Travel.* New York: Popular Library, 1974.

De Chardin, Teilhard, *The Divine Milieu.* New York: Harper & Row, Publishers, 1960.

Ducasse, Curt John, *The Belief in a Life After Death.* Springfield, Ill.: Charles C. Thomas, Publisher, 1951.

Ebon, Martin, ed., *Reincarnation in the Twentieth Century.* New York: World Publishing Company, 1970.

Edmunds, Simeon, *Hypnosis and E.S.P.* N. Hollywood, Calif.: Wilshire Book Company, 1961.

Garrett, Eileen J., *Adventures in the Supernormal.* Toronto, Canada: McClelland & Stewart, Ltd., 1949.

Hollander, Bernard, *Hypnosis and Self Hypnosis.* N. Hollywood, Calif.: Wilshire Book Company, 1957.

Howe, Quincy, Jr., *Reincarnation for the Christian.* Philadelphia: The Westminster Press, 1974.

Ireland, Richard, *The Phoenix Oracle.* New York: Tower Publications, 1970.

Karlins, Marvin, and Andrews, Lewis M., *Biofeedback.* Philadelphia: J. B. Lippincott Company, 1972.

Langley, Noel, *Edgar Cayce on Reincarnation.* New York: Warner Paperback Library, 1967.

LeShan, Lawrence, *The Medium, the Mystic, and the Physicist.* New York: The Viking Press, Inc., 1974.

Lilly, John C., *The Center of the Cyclone.* New York: Julian Press, Inc., 1972.

Maltz, Maxwell, *Psycho-Cybernetics.* Englewood Cliffs, N.J.: Prentice-Hall, Inc., 1960.

Mitchell, Edgar D., and White, John, eds., *Psychic Exploration.* New York: G. P. Putnam's Sons, 1974.

Monroe, Robert A., *Journeys Out of the Body.* Garden City, N.Y.: Anchor Press, imprint of Doubleday & Company, Inc., 1971.

Montgomery, Ruth, *A World Beyond.* New York: Fawcett World Library, 1972.

Naranjo, Claudio, *The One Quest.* New York: The Viking Press, Inc., 1972.

Neff, Richard H., *Psychic Phenomena and Religion.* Philadelphia: The Westminster Press, 1971.

Ornstein, Robert E., *The Psychology of Consciousness.* San Francisco: W. H. Freeman and Company, Publishers, 1972.

Ostrander, Sheila, and Schroeder, Lynn, *Psychic Discoveries Behind the Iron Curtain.* Englewood Cliffs, N.J.: Prentice-Hall, Inc., 1970.

Parker, William R., and Dare, Elaine St. Johns, *Prayer Can Change Your Life.* Englewood Cliffs, N.J.: Prentice-Hall, Inc., 1957.

Rhine, J. B., *New World of the Mind.* New York: William Sloane Associates, 1953.

———, *The Reach of the Mind.* New York: William Sloane Associates, 1947.

Stanford University, *The Dimensions of Healing.* Symposium, Sept. 30–Oct. 4, 1972. Los Altos, Calif.: Academy of Parapsychology and Medicine, n.d.

Stearn, Jess, *The Search for a Soul.* New York: Doubleday & Company, Inc., 1972.

Sugrue, Thomas, *There Is a River.* New York: Holt, Rinehart and Winston, Inc., 1943.

Toffler, Alvin, *Future Shock.* New York: Random House, Inc., 1970.

Ullman, Montague; Krippner, Stanley; and Vaughan, Alan, *Dream Telepathy.* New York: Macmillan Publishing Co., Inc., 1973.

Watson, Lyall, *Supernature.* Garden City, N.Y.: Anchor Press, imprint of Doubleday & Company, Inc., 1973.

Weatherhead, Leslie D., *Psychology, Religion, and Healing.* Nashville: Abingdon Press, 1951.

Weil, Andrew, *The Natural Mind.* Boston: Houghton Mifflin Company, 1972.

White, John, *The Highest State of Consciousness.* Garden City, N.Y.: Doubleday & Company, Inc., 1972.

Whitehead, Alfred North, *Science and the Modern World.* New York: Macmillan, Inc., 1925.

Willingham, Ronald L., *Life Is What You Make It.* Waco, Tex.: Word, Inc., 1973.

Woodward, Mary Ann, *Edgar Cayce's Story of Karma.* New York: Berkeley Publishing Corporation, 1972.

Periodicals

California Living. Weekly magazine of the *San Francisco Examiner and Chronicle,* July 1, 1973.

Intellectual Digest, January, 1973.

————, June, 1973.

————, September, 1973

National Enquirer, October 20, 1973.

————, March 24, 1974.

————, September 24, 1972.

Psychic, July, 1973.

————, February, 1974.

Psychology Today, October, 1973.

San Francisco Chronicle, April 9, 1973.

————, June 25, 1973.

————, September 29, 1973.

Trends; A Journal of Resources, May/June, 1970. Lancaster, Pa.: Geneva Press. Published especially for use by the American Baptist Churches in the U.S.A., The Episcopal Church, The Presbyterian Church in Canada, The United Church of Christ, and The United Presbyterian Church U.S.A.

APPENDIX
A Review of Literature

This appendix contains a review of the main literature used in developing the subject covered in this book. The literature was helpful for information and for ideas. Some of the material shows the history of parapsychology, charting its development. Some of it covers research that is being done, and some of it hypothesizes about the future.

A number of the books deal with evidence that can be considered scientific, that is, containing material that is or has been acquired and accumulated in laboratory settings where sound empirical results can be seen. Other books cannot be used for the validation of the place of parapsychology as a legitimate science but are important as they show different types of literature that are available to readers in the field of parapsychology.

Much of the up-to-date material on this subject is in the form of articles in newspapers, magazines, and other specially printed materials from the different associations involved in parapsychological research. This appendix does not review the articles of periodicals; such material used is in the main body of the book.

Most of the material in these books is not of Christian orientation. But we need to know all of the thinking on the subject before finding our own position.

The books reviewed here can be bought at most book stores that have sections on parapsychology. I recommend the reading of all the books I have included as helpful in acquiring an overall view of the subject matter considered in this book. Each book makes its own particular contribution toward the information and the experience needed for an adequate "feel" of the subject.

Browning, Norma Lee, *The Psychic World of Peter Hurkos.* Garden City, N.Y.: Doubleday & Company, Inc., 1970, 236 pages.

In 14 chapters Norma Lee Browning describes the life of the famous psychic Peter Hurkos. The book is worth reading if one wishes to see the life and development of a psychic who has become very renowned, especially in the area of police work. Browning indicates substantial evidence of certain phenomena. This book's basic value seems to be in the presentation of the "picture of a psychic."

Campbell, Joseph, ed., *The Portable Jung.* Trans. R.F.C. Hull. New York: The Viking Press, Inc., 1971, 659 pages.

Joseph Campbell has drawn from the various writings of Jung the material needed to show the development of Jung's thinking over the range of his life as shown in his writings. Campbell's book is in three parts containing 15 chapters. Of particular interest to the person motivated toward parapsychology are the chapters on the difference between Eastern and Western thinking and on Synchronicity.

Campbell's book shows Jung's thinking on some of the phenomena considered in this book. It is unique and provocative.

Cobb, John B., Jr., *A Christian Natural Theology.* Philadelphia: The Westminster Press, 1965, 288 pages.

In this book Dr. Cobb seeks to interpret and convey the philosophy and teaching of Alfred North Whitehead. He believes Whiteheadian theology can give us a holistic and nonfragmented cosmology that we so desperately need in the Christian world today.

Dane, Christopher, *Psychic Travel.* New York: Popular Library, 1974, 192 pages.

This book is the collection of a number of experiences some people have had with "out of body" travel. There are a number of independent short stories of people leaving their bodies and then coming back to give a recount of their experience.

Ebon, Martin, ed., *Reincarnation in the Twentieth Century.* New York: World Publishing Company, 1970, 128 pages.

This book is assembled by Martin Ebon. It is the account of a number of cases that seem to verify the fact of reincarnation. The stories are well documented and more or less force readers to come up with some kind of an answer for themselves if the stories are verifiable as claimed.

The book indicates some of the persons involved in research in this area, such as Dr. Ian Stevenson, Alumni Professor of Psychiatry, University of Virginia School of Medicine, who is designated as probably the world's outstanding authority on scientific research in reincarnation.

Garrett, Eileen J., *Adventures in the Supernormal.* Toronto, Canada: McClelland & Stewart, Ltd., 1949.

The book is in 21 chapters and is the autobiography of Eileen Garrett as she tells her own experiences as a person with unusual ability. It gives the perspective of a psychic as she first realizes she is "different" and as she seeks to accept and adjust to her abilities. The book also gives some of her concepts of the paranormal and some of her theories about the phenomena occurring in parapsychology.

Howe, Quincy, Jr., *Reincarnation for the Christian.* Philadelphia: The Westminster Press, 1974, 112 pages.

The book is an apologetic for the Christian considering reincarnation as a viable possibility for the theological position he holds. Howe thinks the world's great religions are now rushing toward a convergence of doctrine and practice such as would have been unthinkable at any other time in history. He sees reincarnation as the main difference between Christianity and other religions and believes that this does not need to be so.

Particularly good in my opinion is the chapter dealing with the church. It seeks to account for the treatment of reincarnation by the church, and shows how the church has never really dealt with it as a theological possibility aside from its treatment as presented by Origen of Alexandria. Howe deals with reincarnation as shown in the New Testament.

Ireland, Richard, *The Phoenix Oracle.* New York: Tower Publications, 1970, 167 pages.

The Phoenix Oracle is an autobiography of the psychic life of Richard Ireland. It describes how his ability began to make its powers aware to him, how he developed it and is using it now. You see the "inside life" of the psychic in a good subjective view.

Karlins, Marvin, and Andrews, Lewis M., *Biofeedback.* Philadelphia: J. B. Lippincott Company, 1972.

This is the first comprehensive book on biofeedback. Karlins and Andrews are enthralled by new discoveries in mind-training techniques and present a very stimulating treatment of the subject. The book is a mind-expanding experience, with well-established empirical evidence attesting to the efficacy of biofeedback as one of the most effective methods of training a person to be able to control one's mind. In the back, Karlins and Andrews have included an excellent "Annotated List of Suggested Readings." Since biofeedback is a "laboratory" phenomenon, and thus so credible as to results and process, it is worth reading for scientific support of mind-expanding experiments.

Lilly, John C., *The Center of the Cyclone.* New York: The Julian Press, Inc., 1972, 220 pages.

The Center of the Cyclone is the autobiography of John Lilly's exploration of mind-expanding journeys, seeking to find more meaning than comes from the materialistic world. In 18 chapters the author carries the reader through his experiences with LSD and then other phenomena that opened his awareness to alternate consciousness possibilities.

The book is meaningful to read as an excellent picture of one person's interpretation of mystical experiences with alternate consciousness states. It also shows how John Lilly interprets the different experiences for himself to find meaning and congruence in them for his personal philosophy.

Maltz, Maxwell, *Psycho-Cybernetics.* Englewood Cliffs, N.J.: Prentice-Hall, Inc., 1960, 256 pages.

Psycho-Cybernetics has sold over a million copies and is a classic in terms of the material that emanates from a "positive thinking" approach to the understanding of persons. The author was a plastic surgeon for a number of years. The changes in personality due to changes in appearance inspired a thesis that gave credence to his belief that the most important thing is how persons see themselves. The basic thesis seems to grow out of the conviction that the brain and the nervous system are "neural" parts of the physiology of a person that act at the direction of the person to fulfill the things his/her mind believes. What the person believes about himself or herself needs therefore to be positive.

The book really is dealing with the power of the mind and the influence it has on the success of one's living.

This book demonstrates material that sees the mind as the most important aspect of one's being, the determiner of one's reality, and the creation of the reality in fact. It represents other well-known books that take this same basic approach, such as *How to Win Friends and Influence People; The Power of Positive Thinking;* and *Self Mastery Through Conscious Autosuggestion,* etc.

Mitchell, Edgar D., and White, John, eds., *Psychic Exploration.* New York: G. P. Putnam's Sons, 1974, 708 pages.

Mitchell's book is an extensive overview of the areas of parapsychology being researched by specialists in the different sciences. There are four sections with a total of twenty-nine chapters. This book came out after most of my research had been completed. It was written by many of the leading persons involved in the most current research of parapsychological phenomena today. It is appropriately compiled by Dr. Mitchell. It is a must to read if one wants a picture of the field, and if one wishes to be acquainted with the scientists working in this area of research.

Monroe, Robert A., *Journeys Out of the Body.* Garden City, N.Y.: Doubleday & Company, Inc., 1971, 279 pages.

Monroe seeks to explain and expound on his ability to experience realities that are not physical. He claims to be able to move out of his body (referring to his physical body) into areas he calls Locale two (a second state) and Locale three (a third state). The material is documented from some of his fairly well-kept records. The book explains what is happening, how it seems to happen, how one who is interested can get out of body, and what it possibly means. The conclusions contain some interesting suggestions related to theories of the universe.

The material is supported only by the author's own records so would probably not be of use as scientific data one could consider empirical evidence.

Montgomery, Ruth, *A World Beyond.* New York: Fawcett World Library, 1972, 176 pages.

A World Beyond is the example of what is called "automatic typing." It is worth reading as an example of an alleged outside entity communicating through another person. World-famous psychic Arthur Ford died January 4, 1971. He appeared to the author in her typing, and as she learned to "let her typing go," through her he typed things about the other side. It is very interesting reading and, if it is not true, it shows some very creative material.

Naranjo, Claudio, *The One Quest.* New York: The Viking Press, Inc., 1972, 244 pages.

The One Quest is the work of a psychiatrist and philosopher who is attempting to show the different ways people have sought a higher level of meaning, and how the different ways are really the same way if persons allow themselves to follow the freedom of the leading of their own minds.

The goal of the book seems to be to find unity in multiplicity and from this perspective show the ways, of which he sees many, to the "Great Way of Man." In the author's experiences, in psychotherapy, music, and religion, he concludes that in all three he seems to be doing and seeking the same thing. He searches for a unity in all seeking.

Neff, Richard H., *Psychic Phenomena and Religion.* Philadelphia: The Westminister Press, 1971, 176 pages.

In *Psychic Phenomena and Religion* Richard Neff attempts to be trying to "break the ice" to get Christians to consider other possibilities of belief frameworks for their faith. He, through his wife's and his own experiences, became aware of the world of psychic phenomena. The book is his attempt to understand what the various phenomena mean to himself and to share that meaning with others who might also be seeking. It seems to me to be more of an apologetic. He appears to be rather defensive, probably because of the treatment he has received from some of his Christian friends.

Ornstein, Robert E., *The Psychology of Consciousness.* San Francisco: W. H. Freeman and Company Publishers, 1972, 247 pages.

Ornstein discusses the awareness of the physiological two hemispheres of the brain and makes some psychological suggestions and conclusions as to the difference in the functioning of the two sides.

Ornstein states that he has attempted to stay within that which can be written as science, and also point to a second source of knowledge that comes from the esoteric traditions of the Middle and Far East. He sees these two modes as compatible, even as necessary for a complete or comprehensive understanding of our minds.

Ostrander, Sheila, and Schroeder, Lynn, *Psychic Discoveries Behind the Iron Curtain.* Englewood Cliffs, N.J.: Prentice-Hall, Inc., 1970, 457 pages.

This book is the account of the research about psychic phenomena done by Ostrander and Schroeder while in Iron Curtain countries. It is their report of what they saw and what they experienced as related to the paranormal.

This book gives one an exposure to the different categories of parapsychology; it makes one aware of the tremendous amount of research being done in other parts of the world, seeking to understand and use telepathy, ESP, and other areas found in parapsychology; it shows how much our own country is behind in parapsychological research.

Parker, William R., and Dare, Elaine St. Johns, *Prayer Can Change Your Life.* Englewood Cliffs, N.J.: Prentice-Hall, Inc., 1957, 270 pages.

The 15 chapters of the book show how Dr. Parker developed the emphasis on prayer he had, and reveal the experiments using prayer principles with a class of 45 people from all walks of life.

There is more and more emphasis on prayer and an understanding of it and its effectiveness among parapsychologists. The authors show some of the early explorations of prayer as a therapeutic tool. The experiments are some of the first experiments with prayer, where it is considered to be a reasonable approach to the health of individuals. The authors give in detail the various effects of prayer on the different persons involved in the experimental class. Chapter 4 deals specifically with hypnosis and the power of the mind.

Rhine, J. B., *New World of the Mind.* New York: William Sloane Associates, Inc., 1953, 339 pages.

In *New World of the Mind* Dr. Rhine lets his mind go in order to be philosophical about the whole area of parapsychology. He charts the past, evaluates the present, and suggests the future of the new discovery of PSI.

———, *The Reach of the Mind.* New York: William Sloane Associates, 1947, 235 pages.

This book shows some of the first experiments in parapsychological research by Dr. Rhine. Though it is old, it shows how research began in empirical fashion, and it was Dr. Rhine who probably most influenced other scientists and researchers to do their own further study in this area. The author comes to some definite conclusions about the "extra physical" or "transphysical" nature of man. It is interesting for one interested in the first research projects in parapsychology.

Ullman, Montague; Krippner, Stanley; and Vaughan, Alan, *Dream Telepathy*. New York: Macmillan Publishing Co., Inc., 1973, 300 pages.

The results of scientifically controlled experiments in telepathic dreaming are presented and analyzed in this book. It explains the work of Drs. Montague Ullman and Stanley Krippner, who head the research team at the Dream Laboratory of New York's Maimonides Medical Center Psychiatry Department. The treatment in this subject works from the hypothesis that ESP is more commonly found in the dreaming state than in the conscious. The experiments were over a ten-year period.

The study of dreams seems to be a most respectable place to continue research due to the fact that everyone does dream and thus, if the conclusions of the authors are correct, is psychic. This book is necessary reading if one wishes to be aware of this front line of psychic research.

Watson, Lyall, *Supernature*. Garden City, N.Y.: Anchor Press, imprint of Doubleday & Company, Inc., 1973.

In *Supernature* Watson seeks to give a reasonable explanation for all the phenomena occurring in the activity called the paranormal. Dr. Watson, who is a scientist and author of *The Omnivorous Ape* and *The Living World of Animals,* takes great effort to document all of the things he discusses in the book.

This is a valuable publication for it approaches the paranormal from the viewpoint of a biologist who seems to be looking for a holistic and consistent personal philosophy that fits his scientific training and the things occurring that are nontraditional today.

Weatherhead, Leslie D., *Psychology, Religion, and Healing*. Nashville: Abingdon Press, 1951, 543 pages.

Psychology, Religion, and Healing is a very thorough treatment of the various modes of healing other than the medical mode. It explores these different modes in a critical but often very open way. Leslie Weatherhead researches all possible ways that healing can or might occur and attempts to discuss the phenomena in light of the Christian position. The material is important for the person interested in parapsychological phenomena, due to his dealing with areas now included in the general categories of parapsychology. For example, he discusses hypnotism, the laying on of hands, Christian Science, psychic phenomena (spiritualism), and faith healing.

This book is full of personal examples of the author's own experiences with the various topics mentioned. He is aware of phenomena such as energy transfer, etc., and was willing to consider many things as possibilities that are today being empirically validated.

Weil, Andrew, *The Natural Mind.* Boston: Houghton Mifflin Company, 1972, 229 pages.

In nine chapters Andrew Weil seeks to explore and discuss the issue of drugs. He proposes a theory of why people take drugs and makes some suggestions as to what can be done about the issues of drug use. His basic thesis seems to be that it is natural and healthy for individuals to desire altered states of consciousness. The drug allows one to legitimize for oneself an experience with an altered consciousness state.

The book is important for the person interested in parapsychology, for it presents, as well as I have seen anyone do, a case for the value of letting the mind go to other than objective or controlled mind states. This book gives the person who has never had experiences with altered consciousness by drug use a chance to read of its effects. Andrew Weil shares his experiences freely.

White, John, ed., *The Highest State of Consciousness.* Garden City, N.Y.: Doubleday & Company, Inc., 1972, 484 pages.

The Highest State of Consciousness is a series of essays dealing with the different possibilities of the mind, how one can achieve a more fulfilling or a higher state of being. The essays total thirty-three in number and are by leading men in the field of parapsychology, thereby giving a good overview of the thinking going on in this field. The authors are men like Stanley Krippner, Alan Watts, Charles Tart, Abraham Maslow, and others.

The feeling content of the essays conveys a note of excitement and exploration. A time for opening to new ideas is at hand and it is noticed here. The book is worth reading for a picture of new ideas in thinking.

Whitehead, Alfred North, *Science and the Modern World.* New York: Macmillan, Inc., 1925, 212 pages.

There is a resurgence of interest in Whitehead's philosophy. He lays a foundation for the progressive development of life which, at least for me, provides an overall framework for the setting of things being discussed and evaluated today in the area of parapsychology. I have used many of his general ideas in the last two chapters in particular. Whitehead, in this series of eight lectures, provides the thinking that allows one to conceive of a cosmology, or a holistic view of the universe. The material is very heavy reading.

Woodward, Mary Ann, *Edgar Cayce's Story of Karma.* New York: Berkeley Publishing Corporation, 1972, 256 pages.

The treatment of reincarnation in this book pictures Edgar Cayce as he gave readings for many persons. The seven chapters indicate the logical concepts of reincarnation as one views life as a continuum of progression toward the ultimate of one's becoming and God's program. The book is especially valuable as it presents clearly the concept of *Karma.*